Sex Markets

This is the first study by economists that tackles the complex subject of sex work, which irrespective of its legal status lies at the centre of a globalised service industry, deeply connected with the entertainment and tourism industries as well as with illegal activities. The sheer numbers of human beings involved and the underlying social and policy issues, as well as the revenues generated, demand attention from economists, who, as this book shows, can make a useful contribution to understanding the issues and informing policy design.

The authors begin by presenting a synthesis of the economic and sociological approaches to prostitution and the main feminist debates around the issue. In the second part of the book, they develop an original economic model of the exchange of paid sex including the effect of stigma, which is used to describe the possible consequences from adopting different policy regimes, giving concrete country cases as examples. The final part includes an empirical study of the demand for paid sex that offers empirical support to the model's claims, and points to several possible further research avenues. Whilst retaining many of the assumptions of the economists' toolbox (rational action, representative agents with optimising behaviour, and equilibrium), this work also enriches the economists' approach by considering socially aware agents, that is, individuals who derive both material and immaterial rewards from their actions.

Covering areas such as sex work, trafficking and social stigma, this empirical and mathematically rigorous book is essential reading for students and researchers in the areas of gender economics and gender and development.

Marina Della Giusta is Senior Lecturer in Economics at Reading University Business School, UK.

Maria Laura Di Tommaso is Senior Lecturer in Economics at the Faculty of Political Sciences, University of Turin, Italy.

Steinar Strøm is Professor in Economics at the University of Oslo, Norway, and the University of Turin, Italy.

Routledge IAFFE advances in feminist economics

IAFFE aims to increase the visibility and range of economic research on gender; facilitate communication among scholars, policymakers, and activists concerned with women's wellbeing and empowerment; promote discussions among policymakers about interventions which serve women's needs; educate economists, policymakers, and the general public about feminist perspectives on economic issues; foster feminist evaluations of economics as a discipline; expose the gender blindness characteristic of much social science and the ways in which this impoverishes all research, even research that does not explicitly concern women's issues; help expand opportunities for women, especially women from underrepresented groups, within economics; and, encourage the inclusion of feminist perspectives in the teaching of economics. The IAFFE book series pursues the aims of the organization by providing a forum in which scholars have space to develop their ideas at length and in detail. The series exemplifies the value of feminist research and the high standard of IAFFE sponsored scholarship.

1 Living Wages, Equal Wages
Gender and labor market policies in the United States
Deborah M. Figart, Ellen Mutari and Marilyn Power

2 Family Time
The social organization of care
Edited by Nancy Folbre and Michael Bittman

3 Feminist Economics and the World Bank
History, theory and policy
Edited by Edith Kuiper and Drucilla K. Barker

4 Sexual Orientation Discrimination
An international perspective
Edited by M. V. Lee Badgett and Jefferson Frank

5 The Feminist Economics of Trade
Edited by Irene van Staveren, Diane Elson, Caren Grown, Nilufer Catagay

6 Sex Markets
A denied industry
Marina Della Giusta, Maria Laura Di Tommaso and Steinar Strøm

Sex Markets
A denied industry

Marina Della Giusta, Maria Laura Di Tommaso and Steinar Strøm

LONDON AND NEW YORK

First published 2008
by Routledge
4 Park Square, Milton Park, Abingdon, Oxon OX14 4RN
605 Third Avenue, New York, NY 10017

Routledge is an imprint of the Taylor & Francis Group, an informa business

Typeset in Sabon by Keyword Group Ltd

British Library Cataloguing in Publication Data
A catalogue record for this book is available from the British Library

Library of Congress Cataloging-in-Publication Data
Della Giusta, Marina, 1970–
Sex markets : a denied industry / Marina Della Giusta, Maria Laura Di Tommaso and Steinar Strøm.
p. cm.
Includes bibliographical references and index.
1. Prostitution–Social aspects. 2. Prostitution–Economic aspects. 3. Prostitution–United States. 4. Sex-oriented businesses. I. Di Tommaso, M. L. (Maria Laura) II. Strøm, Steinar. III. Title.
HQ115.D45 2008
363.4'40973–dc22 2007037647

ISBN 13: 978-0-415-39717-9 (hbk)
ISBN 13: 978-0-415-42372-4 (pbk)
ISBN 13: 978-0-203-92950-6 (ebk)

All of us, with the exception of wealthy and unemployed, take money for the use of our body. Professors, factory workers, lawyers, opera singers, sex workers, doctors, legislators – we all do things with parts of our bodies, for which we receive a wage in return. Some people get good wages and some do not; some have a relatively high degree of control over their working conditions and some have little control; some have many employment options and some have very few. And some are socially stigmatised and some are not.

[Martha Nussbaum, *Sex and Social Justice*, 1999]

Contents

Tables and figures

Tables

Figures

Acknowledgements

The authors are grateful to the following publishers and journals for permission to reprint material in this book:

Della Giusta, M., Di Tommaso, M. L. and Strøm, S. (2007). Who is watching? The market for prostitution services. *Journal of Population Economics* (Springer).

Della Giusta, M., Di Tommaso, M. L., Shima, I. and Strøm, S. (2007). What money buys: the demand for prostitution services. *Applied Economics*, Vol. 39. Taylor & Francis Ltd.

Introduction

This book has two ambitions that reflect the series concern: that of being a feminist book which on the basis of the recognition of gender-based and other socially constructed differences studies the inequalities that are justified on their basis; and that of being an economics book, which aims to generate progressive policy prescriptions that redress such inequalities. As the opening quote suggests, we believe that a key characteristic of prostitution is its wide stigmatisation, which depending on the context can affect both sex workers and their clients. We therefore make an explicit effort to include the effect of stigma on individuals in our description of prostitution. Whilst retaining many of the assumptions of the economists' toolbox (rational action, representative agents with optimising behaviour and equilibrium) we also hope to enrich the economists' approach by considering socially aware agents, that is individuals who derive both material and immaterial rewards (and punishments) from their actions. Social construction is therefore at the centre of our approach, and it is presented as the interplay between individual reputations and behaviour and social norms.

With a few notable and noteworthy exceptions (Edlund and Korn, 2002; Cameron et al., 1999; Moffat and Peters, 2001; Cameron, 2002; Cameron and Collins, 2003; Rao et al., 2003; Gertler et al., 2003; Collins, 2004), economists have not studied this form of exchange, in spite of the vast numbers of individuals involved and the connections with other formal and informal economic activities (from the entertainment and tourism industry to organised crime) as well as with the ever more pressing issue of international migration. This book hopes to contribute to filling this gap presenting an empirically grounded study of prostitution as a form of work existing in an economically and socially constructed unequal exchange, and deriving policy suggestions. According to available data and case studies, this is a globalised industry involving millions of workers, characterised by a high degree of inequality in working conditions (ranging from slavery to self managed and legalised unionised employment), by different sub-markets and fully integrated in the productive system. According to a recent survey, in the US 16 per cent of men reported buying sex at least once in their lives, and 0.5 per cent reported doing so at least once a year. In Finland, as in Russia, it was found that 10–13 per cent of men had purchased sex at least once. In Norway, the comparable figure is 11 per cent, in Holland 14 per cent, in Switzerland 19 per cent, in London 7–10 per cent and in Spain 39 per cent. Figures in the 70 per cent range have been recorded for Cambodia and Thailand (Ben-Israel and Levenkron, 2005:13).

Historically the prevailing concern informing policies addressing prostitution has been moral sanctioning of those involved in the trade being directed in different mixtures at sex workers, their clients, or those who organise in a variety of ways the sex trade. Policies addressing prostitution directly or indirectly have also been influenced by women's movements and feminist discourses to a varying degree, as illustrated for example in the discussion of the role of movements and states in the regulation of the sex trade across countries contained in Outshoorn (2004), with the welfare of workers in the sex industry sometimes at the centre of the discussion, although often accompanied by a rather one-sided understanding of their agency (Ward, 2008). As noted earlier, with the exclusion of some recent papers, and the outdated book by Reynolds (1986), which is focused on location (geography of US prostitution markets), economics has largely avoided analysing this phenomenon involving millions of consumers (largely but not exclusively men) and of workers (largely but not exclusively women), although the revenue generated contributes non-negligibly to the economy of many countries (through sex tourism and the connected services and migrants' remittances). This is curious since this is a form of exchange that has many of the features that much recent research in economics claims to want to understand, such as the importance of information and power asymmetries[1] in exchange, the role of regulation in fragmented markets, the relationship between formal and informal markets, women's entrepreneurship, the allocation of resources within the household, the dynamics of international labour mobility, and the pathways out of poverty and social exclusion. There is an unfortunate parallel between the lack of acknowledgement of prostitution as a form of work in policy making and in the economic discipline. Given the relevance of the economic profession to policy makers there is a need for economic research addressing this neglected area of enquiry, learning from the evidence from the sex sector as well as the work carried out in other disciplines.

We begin by presenting a synthesis of philosophical approaches to prostitution, including a discussion of feminist debates around this issue which continue to be heated and reflected in the main opposing policy stances (abolitionism and sex work) which, depending on the degree of influence of feminist agendas on governments, have been variously reflected in concrete policies towards the industry (criminalisation, decriminalisation and legalisation). In terms of policy regimes, we adopt here the definitions used in Outshoorn (2004) whereby abolitionism describes the position according to which prostitution should be banned and third parties criminalised but not sex workers; Prohibitionism means that all prostitution is illegal and parties liable to penalties; and regulation means that the state intervenes in the ways in which the sex industry is run (Outshoorn, 2004; p. 8). It has to be borne in mind that most regulatory regimes have evolved in piecemeal fashion over time, with legislation not explicitly addressing sex work (penal codes reform, public health, social insurance and taxation regimes being the main factors) having an important effect on concrete outcomes.

In Part II we present an economic model of the exchange of paid sex, which belongs to the standard rational action tradition (based on the idea that agents make decisions based on the information available to them and evaluating possible alternatives), but differs in that it contains agents who are social beings interested in varying degrees in the effect of their actions on their reputations, which are socially constructed and affected by what other agents do. The usefulness of economic modelling is that, as long as it is based on valid stylised facts (that is recurrences encountered in empirical evidence), and as long as all simplifying assumptions (especially those relating to *ceteris paribus*, that is the idea that no other factors affecting the model's variables and not included in the model will not change simultaneously with the policy parameters of interest) are borne in mind when discussing the policy implications stemming from the model's results, models can be an extremely useful tool for testing hypotheses, and one whose validity can continuously be checked against empirical evidence. We use our model to describe the possible consequences from adopting different policy regimes, giving concrete country cases as examples.

In Part III we present an empirical study of the demand for paid sex using a dataset containing information on personal characteristics and motivations of clients of street sex workers in the US. According to both official and non-governmental organisation (NGO) estimates, street sex work represents only about 10 to 20 per cent of the prostitution industry, but it is nevertheless extremely important for two reasons: firstly because its visibility has meant that it has often been the focus of media and policy attention, and secondly because it is often regarded, except for trafficking, as the most exploitative part of this business (Kuo, 2002). Using this dataset, we study the role of stigma and the relationship between paid and unpaid sex, and find that these corroborate our model's hypotheses and are in line with findings from other empirical studies. Furthermore, we identify in this sample two diametrically opposite profiles: one for clients whom we label 'experimenters', and one for more experienced ones that we name 'regulars', who have dramatically different attitudes and perceptions of their participation in this activity. We also draw further implications in terms of both policy and future theoretical and empirical research.

Part I

Studying sex work

1.1 Conceptualising sex work

As in the quote at the outset of this book, we share the view of Martha Nussbaum in relation to sex work. The stigma traditionally attached to sex work is based on beliefs that are not defensible, and should be rejected by feminists. Her argument is based on the comparison between many kinds of jobs and sex work. In comparing different uses of the body, she argues that the main difference between prostitution and other jobs is the 'invasion of the sex worker's internal space'. Most of the other differences can be imputed to social stigma and to criminalisation. In order to look better at this issue she gives the hypothetical example of a Colonoscopy Artist: this person uses their skill at tolerating the fibre-optic probe to make a living. It has in common with sex work the consensual invasion of one's bodily space. We would want to ban it or regulate it if we thought it too dangerous, but we would not be moved to ban it for moral reasons. And we would not consider such a person immoral (Nussbaum, 1999).

Sex work has many features in common with other activities entailing bodily service. It differs from these activities in many subtle ways but the biggest difference consists in the fact that it is, today, more widely stigmatised. Feminists are deeply divided on the issue, and the debate between the 'sex-work' and the 'abolitionist' lobbies is often heated and bitter. Those in favour of sex work as a type of work are in favour of a protective legislation that should work at decreasing the social stigma associated with it.

The other feminist view, i.e., the abolitionists, would argue that prostitution can be seen as a perpetuation of the traditional roles of power of men over women and as such should be abolished. According to Pateman what's wrong with prostitution is the perpetuation of a contract where the patriarchal rights of men and women are re-affirmed (Pateman, 1988: 208). So, according to her the difference between workers in a capitalist firm and sex workers is the re-enforcement of a contract that makes the subordination of women publicly recognised. There are however many kinds of jobs where there is a re-enforcement of a contract that makes the subordination of women publicly recognised.

The stigma comes from a moral judgement. Historically, sex work has been seen as immoral because non-reproductive extramarital sex has been viewed as immoral. The stigma can also come because of the connection with gender hierarchy; some feminists have viewed sex workers like veiled women: they are regarded as victims of an unjust system. Nussbaum argues that sex work, when viewed as a complement to marriage, incorporates the stigma as part of the bonds imposed on women's sexuality.

Another important point raised in this debate (see Pateman, 1988 and O'Connell Davidson, 2002) concerns the selling of sexual services as opposed to the selling of the self. The basic idea here is that sex workers do sell sexual services, but not the self. The discussion of Pateman about surrogate mothers sub-contracting their wombs and the similarities she finds with the provision of sexual services, however, leaves some open questions. At the root of the distinction between selling sexual services but not the self is the idea that the acts performed by the body do not affect the perception the individual has of the self or of the body. One could argue that there is not an objective reality: 'the self' or 'the body'. There is the perception each individual has of the self or the body. And this perception is influenced by the acts the body performs. The issue is similar to the one illustrated by Pateman (1988) in which a woman decides to surrogate her womb, but during the pregnancy decides that the 'child is hers'. The fact that her body is changing, that she is feeding the baby, etc. make her rational decision to surrogate her womb vanish. Her sense of self as a mother develops with the pregnancy.[2]

These different points of view also imply different definitions of sex work, as in Carol Pateman (What's wrong with prostitution), Julia O'Connell Davidson[3] (The rights and wrongs of prostitution), or Martha Nussbaum.[4]

The conception of the self is at the centre of Radin's (1996) theoretical approach, which allows us to conceptualise the debate on sex work as a case of contested commodification.[5] Her analysis of contested commodification deals precisely with all those 'instances in which we experience personal and social conflict about the process of commodification and the result', such as prostitution, organs-selling, and baby-selling. Radin argues that personhood is dependent and inseparable from context, in other words many kinds of particulars ('one's politics, work, religion, family, love, sexuality, friendships, ...' p. 56) are integral to the self and it is a violation of humanity to understand them as alienable and monetisable. Social justice needs to confront dilemmas arising from the will to pursue an ideal whilst simultaneously having to deal with present non-ideal circumstances. However, the latter requires compromise and responses that might jeopardise the achievement of the ideal. Radin calls this dilemma the double bind, which in the case of commodification of parts of the self operates as follows: 'First, if we sometimes cannot respect personhood either by permitting sales or by banning sales, justice requires that we consider changing the circumstances that create the dilemma. We must consider power and wealth distribution. Second, we still must choose a regime for the meantime, the transition, in non-ideal circumstances' (p. 124). The double bind is recurrent in feminist struggles as 'a series of dilemmas in which both alternatives are, or can be, losers for the oppressed' (p. 130) so that the only way out of the double bind is through change in the conception of gender. The double bind in women's sex work arises because both commodification (legalisation) and enforced non-commodification (criminalisation) may be harmful: the first by treating essential attributes of persons as fungible objects, the second by denying earning opportunities (or more realistically making the working conditions of illegally working sex workers even worse) in situations of poverty and the lack of alternatives. The removal of oppressive circumstances is the only real solution, but others must be found for the 'transition phase' towards it.

1.2 Social sciences and sex work

The social scientific literature on sex work is vast (recent authoritative monographs on the subject are O'Connell Davidson, 1998, and Lim, 1998) and representative of many different views and concerns. A substantial part of the literature on sex work consists of studies of sex work and its relationship with violence, health and drugs problems, and international migration, and is often devoted to investigating the desirability of alternative regulatory regimes and the definition of rights for sex workers (McKeganey and Barnard, 1996; O'Kane, 2002; Thorbek and Pattanaik, 2002; Doezema, 1998; Tiggey *et al.*, 2000). Whilst studies of sex workers are widespread, those that address the demand side of the industry are harder to come by, and wanting to rigorously analyse demand characteristics on the basis of empirical evidence can prove very difficult:

> Presumably, the client has not been studied until very recently because his actions are not perceived as morally reprehensible. A man who buys sex is viewed simply as a 'man' doing 'what men do' and therefore there is nothing unique or interesting enough about his behaviour to justify research .... For this reason, paid sex is considered legitimate, even 'natural', but part of a private realm that is best left un-discussed.
>
> (Ben-Israel and Levenkron, 2005: 13)

Findings from empirical studies of clients suggest that personal characteristics (personal and family background, self-perception, perceptions of women, sexual preferences), economic factors (education, income, work), as well as attitudes towards risk (health hazard and risk of being caught where sex work is illegal), lack of interest in conventional relationships, desire for variety in sexual acts or sexual partners, and viewing sex as a commodity, are all likely to affect demand. For example, Pitts *et al.* (2004) surveyed a sample of 1225 men and women in Australia[6] and found that 23.4 per cent had paid for sex at least once, and reported paying for sex to satisfy sexual needs (43.8 per cent), because paying for sex is less trouble (36.4 per cent), and because it is entertaining (35.5 per cent). Significantly, they found that there were not many significant differences between men who had paid for sex and those who had not, except that the ones who had were on average older, less likely to have university education and to have had a regular partner in the last year. The motivations of sex workers' clients in the UK (who were all males and appeared to be representatives of all sectors of society) studied in the course of a programme[7] on the sex industry presented by Channel 4 appeared to convey the impression that a connection existed between the effort and costs associated with finding a sexual partner who would readily satisfy their sexual preferences, and the straightforward and readily accessible option of sex work. This is confirmed by Thorbek and Pattanaik (2002), who draw a sort of 'psychological' profile of male sex tourists on the basis of their own descriptions of themselves and accounts of their experiences indicating that many of them are finding relationships with others very difficult (either because they do not have the time or the skills required to meet people) and choose sex tourism as an 'easier' alternative, which does not imply any responsibility towards the person providing the sexual service. As for the views they held of sex workers, it appears that both sexism and racism mix in determining a very marked distancing, which allowed sex tourists to practically ignore and show no interest in the lives and working motivations of the sex workers whose services they buy. Wider phenomena connected to consumerism and globalisation are also clearly related to this industry, which reflects multiple power structures: Marttila (2003) concludes from her study of Finnish clients that: 'the sex business is first and foremost about gendered, economic, social and cultural – global and local – power structures' (Marttila, 2003: 8).

Women clients are also engaging in sex tourism, as documented both in Thorbek and Pattanaik (2002), and in Sanchez Taylor (2001). The latter, in particular, offers a more in-depth analysis of North American and Northern European women buying sex work services of young men in the Caribbean, in what they themselves describe as 'romance holidays'. Responses to her interviews suggest that, on the one hand, women clients are mostly reluctant to define what they engage in as sex work, and, on the other, that their ideas about the young men whose service they buy are deeply rooted in racist ideas about black men and black men's sexuality. The theme of inequality appears to be at the core of the relationship: prejudices that allow the stigmatisation of another person as fundamentally 'different' and inferior to oneself appear again and again in customers' accounts (Ben-Israel *et al.*, 2005; Pitts *et al.*, 2004; Kern, 2000; Blanchard, 1994).

From this literature it emerges that stigma is an important characteristic that we should include in our theoretical model, as is the notion that the demand for paid sex is different from the demand for freely exchanged sex, and incorporates more complex issues which we hope to see reflected in our empirical estimates.

1.3 Economics and sex work

The economic literature has traditionally approached the supply side of the paid sex market either showing how it is similar to other markets, or studying it as a form of crime and analysing the costs and benefits of alternative regulatory regimes, generally agreeing that the main motivation behind supply is an economic one (for a review, see Reynolds, 1986). Recent theoretical and empirical contributions have focussed on modelling prices (Moffat and Peters, 2001; Edlund and Korn, 2002; Cameron, 2002), different types of supply and their determinants (Cameron *et al.*, 1999; Cameron and Collins, 2003), health risk and the effect of condom use on sex worker's earnings (Rao *et al.*, 2003; Gertler *et al.*, 2003), and, more recently, the evolution of paid sex markets and the ways in which urban spaces favour sexual transactions (Collins, 2004). The latter collection is much broader in scope, with paid sex markets being studied as part of the wider sexual market in which people seek partners for reasons that include deficiencies in amount or range of sexual activities in which they participate, or diversification of sexual consumption (Collins, 2004: 1634).

Edlund and Korn (2002) have modelled sex work as a highly paid, low skill female occupation, an alternative to marriage, explaining high wages in terms of a loss of position in the marriage market. Cameron (2002), provides a more sophisticated explanation for high wages in terms of compensation for social exclusion, risk (assault, disease, arrest, punishment), front loading in wage profile (informal pension scheme or insurance), boredom and physical effort, distaste (potential psychological and physical costs), loss of recreational sex pleasure, anti-social and inconvenient hours, possible excess demand and prices used to screen quality, taboos, and agent fees (Cameron, 2002). Moffat and Peters (2001) find that prices are affected by duration of the transaction, location, and age of the sex worker, but that client satisfaction and price paid are affected by different factors. Stigma enters these models in the form of a barrier faced by sex workers when wanting to enter other professions, but it is unrelated to the nature of the transaction between sex worker and client. Cameron and Collins (2003) model males' decision to enter the market for sex work services, where the male has the choice to derive utility from one relationship partner and/or one paid sex partner. They distinguish between the motivations of men in relationships (variety, specific acts, frequency, outlet for stress) and single men ('relative search costs of finding willing sexual partners, or partners willing to engage in specific sexual activities in an *ad hoc* or formal social context, and in a given time period', *ibid.*, p. 274).

Most models to date have shared the assumptions that the object of the sex work transaction is sex, and that sex work is one of the possible ways in which women (and occasionally men) can supply sex to men. Sex work is viewed in these papers as a more or less close substitute to other forms of sexual exchange, and being a man is essential to demanding this service. Biological determinism is used to varying degrees of explicitness and sophistication as the underlying theory of human sexual behaviour, which implies that it is not possible to have a unified economic theory of sex work independent of the sexual identities of the parties involved. Garofalo (2002) is to date the only feminist contribution focussed on explaining the different prices paid in the different sex work sub-markets in terms of the power asymmetries between contractual parties, concentrating on the role of female sex work in the construction of male identity.

Part II

A reputation approach to the analysis of the sex market

This part of the book presents a model of the exchange of paid sex which attempts to incorporate the main stylised facts that derive from empirical evidence and other studies discussed in Part I, and produce results that can be used to simulate different submarkets within the industry, as well as the effect of different regulatory regimes on these submarkets.

Our model is based on two theoretical assumptions which differ from the previous literature; the first is that demand and supply functions do not only depend on sex, but also on the relative social positioning of clients and sex workers.[8]

The second one is that stigma (the opposite of reputation) plays a fundamental role in determining quantities demanded and supplied. By assuming that both sex workers and clients could be male or female, the paper acknowledges on the one hand the fact that, although the overwhelming majority of demand is from males[9] (for both female and male sex workers' services), there is also a female demand (Aggleton, 1998; Sanchez Taylor, 2001). Moreover, the assumption allows us to concentrate on modelling the power aspect intrinsic to the relationship.[10] The power aspect pertains to both gender and variables such as class and race which combine in producing the relative social positioning of sex workers and their clients and play a significant role in stigmatisation (Lim, 1998; Kempadoo *et al.*, 1998; Thorbek and Pattanaik, 2002).

The second important assumption of our model consists of the incorporation of reputation effects in the behaviour of both clients and sex workers. The stigma, associated with both buying and selling, comes from a moral judgement: historically, prostitution has been seen as immoral because non-reproductive extramarital sex has been viewed as immoral (Nussbaum, 1999; Ryley Scott, 1976). In our model both clients and sex workers have potential for reputational losses, which is not affected if they do not engage in sex work. Buying or selling prostitution implies a stigma effect: reducing actual reputation to a lower level then the original potential. We also assume that sex work is a necessary income generating activity, which is rooted in the lack of alternative earning opportunities.

We first look at the sex work market when reputational potentials are exogenous and then we consider the situation when those potentials are considered endogenous. In the endogenous case, it is assumed that if a higher quantity of sex work is sold or bought in the economy, the stigma effect decreases and the corresponding reputational potentials increase.

We discuss the possible implications of different policies and regulatory regimes on the industry and its different markets. Because income is one of the determinants of demand and supply, and given the current unequal distribution of income among gender in most countries (UNDP, 2006), the model predicts the over-representation of men among buyers and women among sellers.

We assume that people care about the effects of their actions on their social standing in the community. This assumption has origin in the economic sociology literature on embeddedness and social capital (Granovetter, 1985; Bordieu, 1986; Coleman, 1988; Putnam, 1993; Mansky, 2000), which points to two distinct ways in which reputations matter to economic agents: firstly because as social beings they derive utility from a positive evaluation by others in the social groups they belong to (Casson, 1991), and secondly because they are aware of the costs that social sanctions may impose on their material progress (Akerlof, 1980; Arnott and Stiglitz, 1991). Reputation has thus both intrinsic and instrumental value: it is desired *per-se* (provider of utility) and can be used to access other earning opportunities. Stigma is a loss of reputation, which can affect pay and working conditions and access to other jobs for sex workers, and can affect clients similarly (depending on the sanctions imposed on them by their community if they are caught). Following Akerlof (1980), we therefore include reputation in agents' preferences. We allow agents to have a different concern for their reputation depending on their personal characteristics and the specific moment at which they exercise choice. We also allow for reputation of the individual to be affected by what others do, here called endogenous norms.

2.1 The demand side, the clients

Let subscript c denote variables related to clients. Let the potential number of clients (as well as the number of sex workers) be equal to 1. Until otherwise stated the model below describes the behaviour of a representative agent. Let:

S_c^0 = sex enjoyed without buying, 'freely exchanged sex'
S_c = amount of sex work bought
C_c = ordinary consumption
I_c = income beyond subsistence level
R_c = capacity for reputation losses of the client when no sex work is bought
w = price of sex work

We assume that the total and exogenous income, I_c, is spent on ordinary consumption and sex. Freely exchanged sex is, by definition, free. We thus have that:

$$C_c = I_c - wS_c. \tag{1}$$

Reputation is reduced when sex is bought in the market. We do not model the probability of being identified as a client and assume that when sex is bought it is also observed in the community. To make things simple we let the clients' realisation for the potential reputation, denoted r_c, be given by equation (2).

$$r_c = R_c - S_c. \tag{2}$$

A low R_c means that clients are vulnerable reputation-wise when buying sex. Therefore a high status individual (politicians, judges) has a low R_c because he is vulnerable reputation-wise. Even a small amount of sex bought (small S_c) can ruin his reputation potential.

A high R_c means that clients have little to lose reputation-wise, i.e., they have a higher capacity for reputation losses. An individual with a low social status may have a high R_c.

A reputation loss can also include the intrinsic feelings of shame and guilt that result from buying sex, especially if the buyer is being unfaithful to a spouse. Thus, we may assume that a married person has a lower reputation capacity (more to lose) than a single person.

We will assume that the utility of the client depends on amount of sex bought, freely exchanged sex, consumption of ordinary goods and reputation, that is:

$$U_c = U_c(S_c, S_c^0, C_c, r_c). \qquad (3)$$

All four marginal utilities are assumed to be positive, which *inter alia* means that the higher the capacity for reputation losses is, the higher the utility. From equation (3) we note that paid sex and freely exchanged sex may be substitutes from a client's point of view. This does not preclude the existence of people for whom these are two very distinct types of goods. We will assume that the agent is maximizing utility, given the budget constraint. In what follows, and to keep things simple, we will assume that the amount of freely exchanged sex, S_c^0, is given and thus is constant. First, we establish the conditions for entry in the market for a client. Inserting from equation (1) and (2) in equation (3) and maximizing with respect to S_c yields the following condition for participating in the sex market:

$$\left[\frac{\partial U_c/\partial S_c}{\partial U_c/\partial C_c}|S_c = 0\right] \geq w + \left[\frac{\partial U_c/\partial r_c}{\partial U_c/\partial C_c}|S_c = 0\right] + \tau_c. \qquad (4)$$

The client will participate in the sex market if his willingness to pay for the first unit of prostitution (left-hand side in equation (4)) exceeds the price of prostitution (w), plus the marginal costs of a worsened reputation for consuming it for the first time (the second term on the right-hand side in equation (4)) and a threshold level τ_c which is positive at $S_c = 0$ and zero otherwise. We thus assume that there is a discontinuity in the utility function such that loss in reputation incurred from consuming the first 'unit' of commercial sex is greater than that incurred from consuming subsequent 'units'. The entry into the market then implies a threshold crossing; see Cameron (2002). The threshold level may depend on individual characteristics as well as on neighbourhood characteristics.

Given that equation (4) holds, then the first-order condition for consuming paid sex is given by:

$$\frac{\partial U_c/\partial S_c}{\partial U_c/\partial C_c} = w + \frac{\partial U_c/\partial r_c}{\partial U_c/\partial C_c}. \tag{5}$$

Equation (5) states that at utility maximum the marginal willingness to pay for sex (in terms of consumption of ordinary goods) should be equal to the price of sex plus the marginal cost of a worsened reputation (in terms of consumption of ordinary goods).

To obtain more specific results we will assume the following functional form of the utility function:

$$U_c = \alpha_0(S_c^0) + \alpha_1 S_c + \alpha_{11} S_c^2 + \alpha_2 C_c + \alpha_3 r_c + \alpha_{33} r_c^2 + \alpha_4 C_c S_c - \tau_c. \tag{6}$$

Thus, we postulate utility as quadratic in consumption of sex and reputation and linear in consumption of ordinary goods, but we allow for an interaction between consumption C_c and commercial sex, S_c. The functional relationship for how freely exchanged sex enters utility is not specified, but we note that from our specification freely exchanged sex and prostitution are not substitutes. To bring in this substitution is straightforward. The threshold function is such that for $S_c = 0$, $\tau_c > 0$ and for $S_c > 0$, $\tau_c = 0$. Actually what we do to keep things simple is that:

$$\left[\frac{\partial \tau_c}{\partial S_c}\bigg| S_c = 0\right] = \tau_c.$$

From Equations (4), (5) and (6) we now get:

$$S_c > 0, \quad \text{if } a_1 + a_4 I_C \geq w + (a_3 + a_{33} R_C) + \tau_c. \tag{7}$$

where:

$$\left\{a_1 = \frac{\alpha_1}{\alpha_2},\ a_{11} = \frac{2\alpha_{11}}{\alpha_2},\ a_3 = \frac{\alpha_3}{\alpha_2},\ a_{33} = \frac{2\alpha_{33}}{\alpha_2},\ a_4 = \frac{\alpha_4}{\alpha_2}\right\}. \tag{8}$$

Here a_1, a_3 and a_4 are all positive,[11] and in order to have a quasi-concave utility function the following must hold:

$$a_{11} + a_{33} < 0 \tag{9}$$

with $a_{11} < 0$ the marginal utility of consuming paid sex is diminishing with consumption, given reputation. If $a_{33} < 0$, the marginal utility of a higher reputation capacity declines with the size of this capacity. Note, however, that it is not necessary for the quasi-concavity of the utility function that both these two parameters are negative, only the sum of them has to be negative.

Provided $a_{33} < 0$, we observe from equation (7) that the higher the reputation capacity, R_c, is, the lower is the marginal cost from reputation effects of consuming sex, and the more likely it is that sex is consumed. The lower threshold level, τ_c, the less serious is the threshold crossing problem and the more likely it is that the individual will enter the market. We also observe that the higher the income, I_c, is and the lower the price, w, is the higher is the chance that the individual will enter the market.

Given that S_c is positive, the demand for paid sex is given by:

$$a_1 + a_{11}S_c + a_4I_c - 2a_4wS_c = w + a_3 + a_{33}r_c. \qquad (10)$$

From equation (10) we can derive the demand for paid sex as a function of the price of sex and reputation capacity. However, to describe the demand curve it is more convenient to consider the price w as a function of the amount of sex bought, S_c. We thus get:

$$w = \frac{(a_1 - a_3) - a_{33}R_c + a_4I_c + (a_{11} + a_{33})S_c}{1 + 2a_4S_c}. \qquad (11)$$

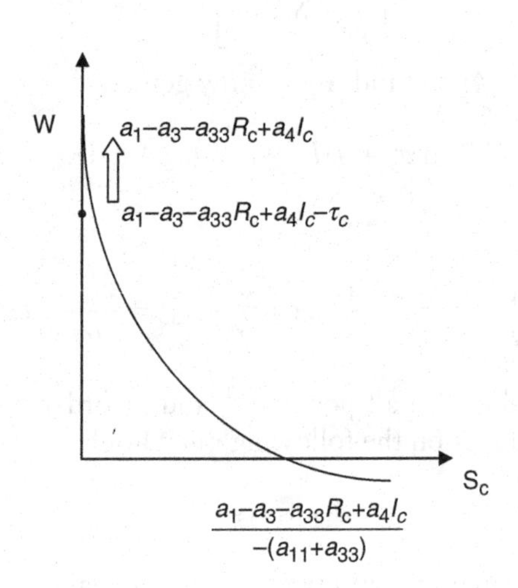

Figure 1 Demand

The derivative of this demand function is given by:

$$\left.\begin{aligned}\frac{\partial w}{\partial S_c} &= \frac{a_{11}+a_{33}-2a_4w-\tau_c}{1+2a_4S_c}; \quad S_c=0\\ \frac{\partial w}{\partial S_c} &= \frac{a_{11}+a_{33}-2a_4w}{1+2a_4S_c}; \quad S_c>0.\end{aligned}\right\} \tag{11'}$$

From (11′), the demand for paid sex is a downward sloping function of price, provided that the utility function is strictly quasi-concave, that is $(a_{11}+a_{33})<0$. The demand function has a jump upwards at $S_c=0$. It is straightforward to show that the demand function is convex, that is curved towards the origin. To have a positive demand it is required that $(a_1-a_3-a_{33}R_c+a_4I_c)>0$.

The demand curve is shifted upwards when the capacity for reputation losses as well as the income is shifted upwards. We also note that when the demand curve is shifted upwards the more utility the agent derives from having sex (a_1 higher) and/or the lower the utility loss is through reputation losses (a_3 lower). The demand curve is shown in Figure 1.

2.2 The supply side

Subscripts p denote variables related to sex workers. The amount of sex sold reduces both leisure and reputation for sex workers. To make things simple we measure reputation and leisure in the same units as sex sold. Let H_p denote hours available for work in sex market above those worked elsewhere. So if H_p is high, sex workers have few other options than selling sex; if it is low, sex workers have many other options. To capture the labour supply effects without a detailed modelling of labour supply in ordinary jobs we assume that H_p depends on income I_p in ordinary jobs. The higher this income is, the higher is labour supplied in ordinary jobs, and the less attractive it is to work as a sex worker. Leisure, denoted L_p, thus depend on income in ordinary jobs, that is $L_p = H_p(I_p) - S_p$, where the derivative of H_p is negative. Sex workers derive utility from consumption of goods and services, C_p, which is financed by total income $I_p + wS_p$, where wS_p is the income from selling sex. Let R_p denote the reputation capacity of the sex worker. A high R_p means that sex workers have little to lose reputation-wise when selling prostitution and a low R_p means the opposite. The actual reputation is denoted $r_p = R_p - S_p$.

The utility is given by:

$$U_p = U_p(L_p, C_p, r_p). \tag{12}$$

The utility function as well as the availability of ordinary jobs and reputation capacity may vary across individuals. All three marginal utilities are assumed to be positive. Again, we have to start with the condition for participating at all as a sex worker. Assuming that the agent is maximizing utility with respect to offering sex services, we get the following participation criteria:

$$S_p > 0 \text{ if } \left[\frac{\partial U_p/\partial L_p}{\partial U/\partial C_p}|S_{p=0}\right] \leq w - \left[\frac{\partial U_p/\partial r_p}{\partial U_p/\partial C_p}|S_p = 0\right] - \tau_p. \quad (13)$$

Thus, an individual will start to sell sex if the price for selling the first amount of sex (w), minus the costs of a worsened reputation for doing so (the second term to the right in equation (13)) and minus the threshold level related to entry as in the case of clients, measured in the same units as w, τ_p, exceeds the shadow price of leisure evaluated at zero prostitution sold. Given that the individual participates as a seller, the optimal amount of sex sold is determined by the following condition (together with the hours and budget constraints):

$$\frac{\partial U_p/\partial L_p}{\partial U/\partial C_p} = w - \frac{\partial U_p/\partial r_p}{\partial U_p/\partial C_p}. \quad (14)$$

Thus, at optimum the shadow price of leisure (the term to the left in equation (14)) equals the marginal net gain of supplying labour through the sale of sex. This marginal net gain equals the price of sex obtained in the market minus the shadow price of reputation.

Again to proceed with more specific results we will assume that the utility function of the sex worker can be specified as:[12]

$$\begin{aligned} U_p = {} & \beta_1(H_p(I_p) - S_p) + \beta_{11}(H_p(I_p) - S_p)^2 + \beta_2(I_p + wS_p) \\ & + \beta_3(R_p - S_p) + \beta_{33}(R_p - S_p)^2 - \tau_p. \end{aligned} \quad (15)$$

Let:

$$\left\{b_1 = \frac{\beta_1}{\beta_2};\ b_{11} = \frac{2\beta_{11}}{\beta_2};\ b_3 = \frac{\beta_3}{\beta_2};\ b_{33} = \frac{2\beta_{33}}{\beta_2}\right\}. \quad (16)$$

A necessary condition for the utility function to be quasi-concave is that $b_{11} + b_{33} < 0$. Again a sufficient condition for this is to assume that both the marginal utility of leisure is diminishing in leisure enjoyed and the marginal utility of reputation is declining in the level of reputation. Each of them will be negative. This will be assumed here. The mathematical property of τ_p is similar to τ_c above.

We now have:

$$S_p > 0, \text{ if } b_1 + b_{11}H_p(I_p) \leq w - (b_3 + b_{33}R_p) - \tau_p. \quad (17)$$

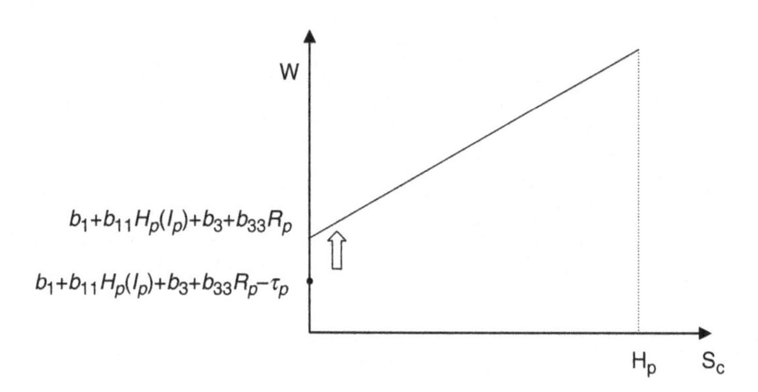

Figure 2 Supply

We observe that the higher the price, w, of sex is and the lower the income in an ordinary job, I_p, is the more likely it is that an individual will supply sex. Moreover, the more it takes to ruin one's own reputation (the larger R_p) the more likely it is that prostitution will be sold. The less serious the threshold crossing problem is the more likely it is that the individual will start working as a sex worker.

Given that $S_p > 0$, then the optimal amount of paid sex can be derived from the following supply function:

$$w = b_1 + b_{11}H_p(I_p) + b_3 + b_{33}R_p - (b_{11} + b_{33})S_p. \qquad (18)$$

The supply curve is an upward sloping linear curve and it is given in Figure 2.

If the capacity for reputation losses, R_p, increases, the supply curve is shifted downwards. This means that at a given price of paid sex, the sex worker is willing to supply more. A higher value for R_p means that more sex can be sold without destroying ones' own reputation. The same type of shift will occur if I_p gets lower (H_p gets higher), which means that if a person has fewer other working possibilities than sex work, they will be willing to offer more paid sex, given the price and the characteristics of the individuals.

We will now turn to market equilibrium, when both clients and sex workers participate in the market. To begin with, we simplify matters and ignore heterogeneity, but in Section 2.3 we will discuss the implications for the model of going beyond the representative agents.

2.3 Market equilibrium

At market equilibrium the price of sex as seen from the demand side has to be equal to the price of sex as seen from the supply side. The amount of sex sold has to be the same, here denoted S^*.

From equations (11) and (18) we then get:

$$S^* = f(H_p(I_p), R_p, R_c) \tag{19}$$

where f is a function increasing in H_p, that is decreasing in I_p, increasing in R_p and R_c. A closed form solution for the equilibrium of sex sold is a little messy but straightforward. The equilibrium wage w^* then follows from either equation (11) or equation (18). In Figure 3 we show the equilibrium and we note that there is a unique equilibrium.
The unnumbered table below describes the impact of changes in the key parameters on the equilibrium price and quantity of paid sex.

Changes in S^* and w from increases in $\{R_c, R_p, I_p\}$

Change in	R_c	R_p	I_p
S^*	+	+	−
W	+	−	+

Column 2 shows that more paid sex is sold at a higher price when the reputation capacity of clients increases, and/or when clients are able to cover to a great extent their consumption of paid sex.

Column 3 suggests that if it becomes more difficult to have one's reputation ruined by being found out as a sex worker, then more paid sex will be sold at a low price. This is consistent with the evidence of some temporary immigrant sex workers in Europe who aim to work in the sex market only for a limited amount of time to accumulate

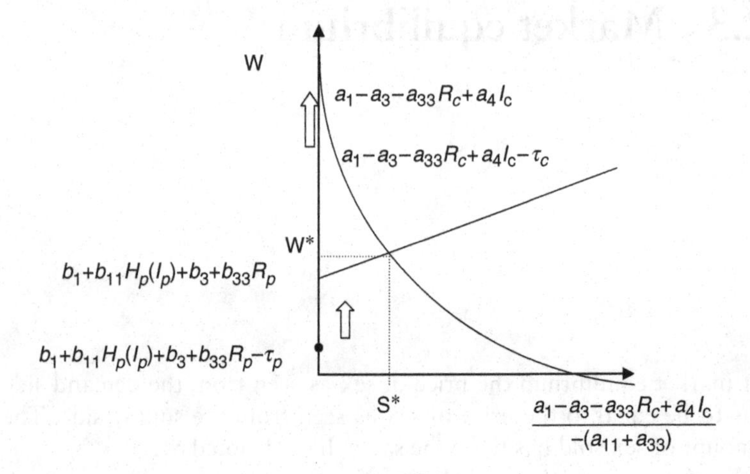

Figure 3 Equilibrium

savings and then return to their country (see Thorbek and Pattanaik, 2002; Corso and Trifirò, 2003).

Column 4 states that the higher the income in an ordinary job is (H_p lower), the less paid sex is sold at a higher price. This implies that an improvement in labour market opportunities for the possible sex workers may reduce paid sex.

Note that the price of paid sex at equilibrium may reflect compensation in terms of reputation losses among clients as well as sex workers, thus our analysis has much in common with Cameron (2002).

2.4 The sex market when norms are endogenous

In the preceding sections we assumed that the reputation capacities were exogenously given and considered only demand and supply for representative agents on both sides of the market. Here we will relax the first assumption. Because of this, we also have to consider demand, supply and equilibrium for the population as a whole. We will not, however, introduce any heterogeneity in the model, which of course has to be done in empirical specifications. To simplify exposition we let the total number of clients and sex workers be the same and equal to N, and without loss of generality we set $N = 1$.

According to Akerlof's theory of social custom (Akerlof, 1980), the fact that people may tend to generally believe or disregard any social code, and the existence of a range of social codes, together may imply that multiple equilibria exist, each corresponding to a different social code. In our context sex work is stigmatised in different degrees in different societies, and changing social attitudes towards it can therefore be expected to produce different market equilibria.

The reputation function in Akerlof depends on the individual's obedience of the code and the proportion of the population who believe in that code. Similarly, in our model we assume that the larger the market for sex work, the more it will take for a single agent to ruin his or her own reputation supplying or consuming sex services. We therefore assume that reputation depends on the number of clients and sex workers, respectively. Thus the larger the proportion of the population that is engaged in sex work, the less stigmatisation and therefore the higher reputation capacities, i.e. that it takes more to ruin ones' reputation. In our representative agent framework we then have

$$R_c = NS_c = S_c, \tag{20}$$

$$R_p = NS_p = S_p. \tag{21}$$

When the agents make their choice, we do not assume that they take equations (20) and (21) into account. The impact of individual sexual behaviour on the norms in the society has the character of externalities.

From equations (11) and (20) we now get the following demand curve, provided that S_c is strictly positive:

$$w = \frac{(a_1 - a_3) + a_4 I_c + a_{11} S_c}{1 + 2a_4 S_c}. \tag{22}$$

From equations (11) and (22), we note that the downward sloping demand curve for sex has now been twisted around. It starts lower on the w-axis[13] and the slope is numerically lower (see Figure 4).

From equations (18) and (21) we get:

$$w = b_1 + b_{11} H_p(I_p) + b_3 - b_{11} S_p. \tag{23}$$

Again, by comparing equations (18) and (23) we observe that the supply curve now starts higher up on the w-axis[14] and the slope is lower.

Let S^{**} denote the equilibrium level of aggregate sex sold in the market. From equations (22) and (23) we obtain

$$S^{**} = g(I_c, H_p(I_p)). \tag{24}$$

Provided that sex workers and clients have entered the market, we observe that at equilibrium the amount of sex sold depends on the income of the clients and the income in other jobs for the sex workers. It can easily be shown that at equilibrium the amount of sex sold, S^{**}, and the price of buying sex, w^{**}, is increasing with the income of the client, whereas the amount of sex sold is decreasing with the income in other jobs of the sex workers and the price is increasing with this income. Thus in countries with an uneven income distribution and discrimination in the labour market, where the clients typically are rich and the possible sex workers are poor, we should expect more sex sold at lower prices, compared to societies where income and job opportunities are more evenly distributed. In these latter countries relatively less sex is sold and prices are higher. Given the taste for prostitution, one should hence expect that there are commercial interests tied to importing possible sex workers to rich countries. Other things being equal, this result also points to a policy measure against prostitution: by improving the quality and availability of other job opportunities, we would expect a decline in the equilibrium amount of sex sold.

The equilibrium when reputation capacity is endogenous, together with the equilibrium when the capacities are treated as exogenous, is given in Figure 4. Comparing the different types of equilibria we note that the impact on the price of paid sex services as well as the amount of sex sold is ambiguous. Figure 4 illustrates some possible outcomes.

We can distinguish between four different equilibria:

1 The reputation capacities are exogenous. The 'interpretation' is that the actions of the agents are not able to change moral standards. They are absolute and given. In this case an amount of sex work sold is S_A and the price is w_A. This equilibrium may serve as the benchmark case (Point A in Figure 4).
2 The clients' reputation capacity increases with how much sex is sold. Reputations of the sex workers' are not affected by the amount of sex sold. More paid sex is sold and the price is higher than in the benchmark case (Point B in Figure 4).
3 The sex workers' reputation capacity is affected by what the sex workers do, but this is not the case for clients. Less paid sex is sold at a higher price compared to the benchmark case (Point C in Figure 4).
4 Both the clients' and the sex workers' reputation capacities are affected by what these two parties do. Less amount of prostitution

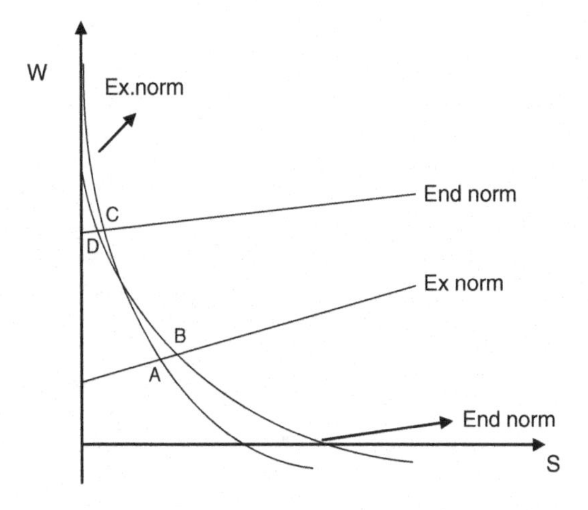

Figure 4 Equilibrium with endogeous and exogeneous norms

is sold at a higher price as in the benchmark case (Point D in Figure 4).

The main reason for the two latter results is that the shadow price of leisure gets higher at equilibrium and the sex workers demand a higher price to be willing to sell sex services.

2.5 Different markets and policies

Decriminalisation, criminalisation, abolitionism

As stated at the outset of the book, regulatory regimes have often been formulated with the most visible parts of the industry in mind, and concrete policies of course include much more than just the legal framework within which the activity occurs, and cover all ways in which governmental activities affect sex markets (social, medical, psychological and educational support): as pointed out in Kuo (2002), the failure to support legal prescriptions with real service provision is of particular concern to the feminist, as women have often been the recipients of progressive policy pronouncements that were never backed up with concrete policy commitments, which have been marginalised from spending decisions and left to the non-governmental sector (for an interdisciplinary perspective on the regulation of prostitution see Munro and Della Giusta, 2008).

In the light of the examples above, policies that were to recognise sex work as a job and reduce the associated stigma would have the effect of increasing the marginal net gain of supplying sex work, and increase the marginal willingness to pay for sex. This should, in a closed economy, have the effect of increasing the price of sex and, given the same availability of alternative earning opportunities and if there are constant intermediation margins, also increase the quantity supplied. However, in an open economy there always is immigration of illegal workers and out-migration of clients (sex tourism), which would help keep prices low.

Policies that increase the stigma of being clients, conversely, increase the costs associated with being caught. This has been done with the expectation that it would reduce the marginal willingness to pay and therefore the quantity of sex sold as well as the equilibrium price. However, the evidence from countries that criminalise clients seems to suggest that clients may try to invest in strategies that reduce the risk of being caught rather than reducing their demand.

Another strategy followed by intervention programmes has been that of increasing alternative earning opportunities for sex workers. The effect of these policies will be felt only on that part of sex work which is supplied for lack of earning alternatives, which implies a fall in part of the supply which will not affect demand and therefore in an open economy setting might simply generate displacement of demand, rather than less prostitution being sold at a higher price.

Clearly the effect of policies also depends on the particular segment of the industry that is being addressed, and our model allows the description of up to 32 different markets within the prostitution industry, depending on clients' reputation and their concern for it, and sex workers' employment alternatives, their reputation and concern for it.

Taking the demand side first, recall that a high a_1 means that the client is less concerned about reputation and a low a_1 means the opposite. Moreover, a high R_c means that clients have little to lose reputation wise when having paid prostitution, and a low R_c the opposite. Then let $F_c(i, j)$ mean a combination of $i = H, L$ and $j = H, L$, for example (a_1 high, R_c low). Then there are four combinations:

$$\{F_c(H,\ H), F_c(H,\ L), F_c(L,\ H), F_c(L,\ L)\}. \tag{27}$$

For example, $F_c(H, L)$ may be a careless judge, who has much to lose if caught purchasing prostitution.

Now consider the supply side. For sex workers, recall that a high b_1 means a relative preference for more leisure and less concern for reputation, and a low b_1 the opposite. Also, a high R_p means that sex workers have little to lose reputation-wise when selling prostitution and a low R_p the opposite. Furthermore, a high H_p indicates that sex workers have few other options than selling sex, and a low H_p indicates many other options than selling sex. Again, let $F_p(k, r, s)$ mean a combination of $k, r, s = H, L$ for example (b_1 high, H_p low, R_p low), so that all together there are eight different cases for sex workers. For example a student who prefers leisure and who is not concerned about their reputation, but has a lot of other options other than selling sex, and little to lose reputation-wise by selling sex far from their environment will have $F_p(H, L, H)$.

Matching the cases generates 32 different possibilities, which can potentially describe 32 different markets, or particular cases. A careless judge purchasing sex services from a student would be the combination $F_c(H, L)$ and $F_p(H, L, H)$. The price of sex work will be high and the amount sold will be low compared to the reference case of $F_c(H, H)$ and

$F_p(L, H, H)$, which could describe average status clients not concerned about their reputation, purchasing street sex work, where street sex workers typically have few other jobs available and do not enjoy very high social status. This standard market relative to the others will have the lowest price and the highest amount of sex work sold.

Despite the lack of a gendered demand and supply, our model predicts the current over-representation of women among suppliers and men among demanders. This follows directly from the inclusion of income in the utility function of clients and sex workers. The model predicts that the higher the income of the sex worker in ordinary jobs, the lower the hours available for working in prostitution and therefore the less prostitution is sold at a higher price. Given that in all the countries in the world (see UNDP, 2006), the income earned by women is less than the income earned by men (even in countries with low gender inequality, Norway for instance, the wage gap is around 20 per cent), our model predicts the current situation where women supply and men demand. But it allows also for the opposite situation, where rich Western women demand prostitution services from men in developing countries. In other words, assuming a model of sex work based on different power between sex workers and clients allows us to stress the importance of income in determining inequality, and explains the observed gendered distribution of demand and supply without the need for biological determinism.

Our analysis sheds light on many issues that have so far remained formally unconnected in economic analysis, and given the present reviews of sex work policies taking place across several countries, hopefully will attract more economists to produce work that can be usefully applied to policy formulation.

Part III

Empirical application

3.1 The demand side

Clients of street sex workers in the US

3.1.1 Description of the data

The dataset contains background characteristics, attitudes and reported behaviours of arrested male clients of female street sex workers in four US cities (San Francisco, Portland, Las Vegas, Santa Chiara) over the period 1996–1999 (Monto, 2000a). The data was collected in the context of two client intervention programmes aiming to address the male demand side of sex work: Portland's Sexual Exploitation Education Project and San Francisco's First Offender Prostitution Program, both aiming at prevention efforts with clients, rather than with sex workers.[15]

Clients who were caught at the moment of paying a street sex worker and arrested were asked to participate in the San Francisco's First Offender Prostitution Program followed by similar initiatives in Santa Clara and Fresno, California and Las Vegas, Nevada. The one-day workshop aimed to instruct the arrested clients about the legal, social and health-related consequences of engaging in sex work and endow them with persuasive reasons to not rehire sex workers. The program considers sex work as an institution built on violence, sexual exploitation, poverty and misogyny. The participation of the arrested clients in this programme allowed them to be dismissed by their crime against a US$500 fee. The Portland programme was a 15-hour, weekend workshop administered by an independent organisation in cooperation with the District Attorney's Office. Some of the men participating in the programmes were required to do so as part of their sentence, others had reduced fines or the arrest purged from their records in exchange for their attendance. Arrested clients of street sex workers who agreed to participate in an intervention programme compiled a detailed anonymous self-administered questionnaire. Over 80 per cent of participants completed the questionnaires, resulting in a sample of 1342 individuals.[16]

The data collection process implies three levels of selection:

(1) The individuals in the data set are those who were caught. We are not able to check if the arrested clients' characteristics are similar or different from those who were not caught. We can speculate on possible correlations between being a regular client and the ability of not being caught but we are not able to measure the possible bias generated by this first selection.
(2) The individuals in the data set are those who participate in the rehabilitation programme. We do not have information on those clients who did not participate.
(3) The individuals in the data set are those who, being arrested and participating in the rehabilitation programme, did complete the questionnaire.

These three selection levels introduce a bias in our analysis. Arrested clients could be on average less experienced in buying sex from street sex workers than non-arrested clients and therefore end up being caught. Moreover arrested clients motives for seeking sex workers could be different from those who were not caught. Here we do not deal explicitly with selection bias issues, which we leave for future work.

Table 1 compares the sample of clients with a National sample taken from the National Health and Social Life Survey, conducted in 1992, using a nationally representative sample[17] which contains extensive information on the US population aged 18–59 able to complete an interview in English.

Comparing our sample with the national survey, we note an under-representation of whites relative to other ethnic groups. On average, our clients are slightly older than the national sample and more of them are not married relative to in the national sample. They also have unhappier marriages, more sex-partners compared to the national sample, lower frequencies of sex during the 12 months prior to the interview, and are on average better educated compared with the national sample: 71 per cent have at least some college after high-school, against 35 per cent nationally. Labour force participation is similar to the national sample.

In our sample, 27 per cent of respondents claimed that they had never had sexual relations with a sex worker (see Table 2).[18] The most common circumstance of the first encounter with a sex worker was being approached by a sex worker (33 per cent), followed by

Table 1. Characteristics of arrested clients

Variable description	*Responses of arrested clients*	*National sample*
Race		
White	57.7%	84.6%
Black or African American	5.2%	10.6%
Other	37.2%	4.8%
Observations total	1313 = 100%	1463 = 100%
Education		
Didn't graduate high school	10.5%	12.1%
Graduated high school	18.4%	52.3%
College after high school	36.3%	6.9%
Received bachelor's	24.2%	18.8%
Received a master's	10.7%	9.9%
Observations total	1329 = 100%	1460 = 100%
Labour force status		
Working full time	82.9%	77.1%
Working part time	5.9%	8.1%
In school	2.2%	3.3%
Unemployed/laid off	4.4%	5.4%
Other	4.6%	6.1%
Observations total	1275 = 100%	1463 = 100%
Average age of arrested clients	(mean = 38, min = 18 and max = 84)	
Age 18–25	12.7%	14.4%
Age 26–35	33.1%	31.6%
Age 36–45	31.1%	31.2%
Age >46	23.2%	22.8%
Observations total	1248 = 100%	1463 = 100%
Marital status		
Married	42.2%	55.8%
Widowed	1.6%	0.8%
Divorced	14.9%	11.9%
Separated	6.4%	2.4%
Never married	34.9%	29.1%
Observations total	1328 = 100%	1463 = 100%

Table 1. Cont'd

Marriage description		
Very happy	37.9%	59.7%
Pretty happy	40.3%	37.9%
Not too happy	21.8%	2.4%
Observations total	528 = 100%	809 = 100%
Sex partners last year		
0 partners	9.9%	10.1%
1 partner	37.6%	70.9%
2 partners	16.7%	8.2%
3–4 partners	17.0%	7.4%
More than 5 partners	18.8%	3.4%
Observations total	1315 = 100%	1349 = 100%
Frequency of sex during last 12 months		
Not at all	10.3%	9%
Once or twice	9.1%	6.4%
Once a month	15.3%	10.9%
3 times per month	21.3%	18.5%
Once a week	19.2%	21.7%
2–3 times per week	17.7%	25.1%
More than 3 times per week	7.2%	8.4%
Observations total	1268 = 100%	1317 = 100%

Note: Total percentage values may not equal 100 per cent due to rounding of numbers.

'approached the sex worker on my own' (30 per cent), and 'a group of buddies set me up' (24 per cent). The most frequent sexual act done with the sex worker was oral sex (54 per cent), followed by vaginal sex (14 per cent). As far as risk is concerned, 74 per cent of the sample declared that they always used a condom (for more details see Table 2).

Arrested clients were asked to agree or disagree with 13 statements designed to reflect popular and scholarly understandings of the reasons men seek out sex workers. Many findings from other studies are supported by these results, which indicate clearly that demand for paid sex and free sex are not perfect substitutes.

From the responses, it can be observed that a considerable number of clients appear to be excited by the illicit, risky, or different quality of sex with a sex worker. Some men pay for sex because they have difficulty becoming involved in relationships, and for some of these men sex work is an attempt not only to have sex, but also to establish intimate

Table 2. Attitudes towards sexual behaviour

Variable description	*Responses of arrested clients*
Circumstances when first with sex workers	
Were approached by sex workers	32.7%
They approached the sex workers on their own	29.7%
A group of buddies set them up	23.9%
Other	5.1%
Family member or relatives set them up	4.5%
Brothel	2.9%
Military	1.2%
Total observations	1040 = 100%
Mostly done with a sex worker	
Oral sex	53.6%
Vaginal sex	14.4%
Checked more than two acts	17.8%
Half and half	10.5%
Other	3.7%
Total observations	911 = 100%
Condom use with sex workers	
Always use it	74.2%
Often	11.7%
Sometimes	7.1%
Never use it	4.2%
Seldom	2.8%
Total observations	1024 = 100%
Sex with sex workers during last 12 months	
Never	26.8%
Only one time	26.7%
More than 1 time but less than once per month	34.6%
1 to 3 times per month	9.3%
Once or 2 times per week	1.7%
3–4 times per week	0.4%
5 or more times per week	0.5%
Total observations	1054 = 100%

Table 3. Motives for seeking sex workers

	Agree strongly and agree somewhat (%)	*Disagree strongly and disagree somewhat (%)*	*Total (%)*	*Total observations*
Difficulty meeting women who are not nude dancers or sex workers	23	77	100	1244
Think most women find me unattractive physically	24	76	100	1248
Want different kind of sex than regular partner	41	59	100	1237
Shy and awkward when try to meet a woman	41	59	100	1246
Have sex with a sex worker than have a conventional relationship with a woman	18	82	100	1244
Excited by the idea of approaching a sex worker	43	57	100	1244
Don't have the time for a conventional relationship	32	68	100	1239
I don't want the responsibilities of a conventional relationship	28	72	100	1233
Like to have a variety of sexual partners	41	59	100	1244
Like to be in control when I'm having sex	42	58	100	1232
Like to be with a woman who likes to get nasty	52	48	100	1230
Need to have sex immediately when aroused	31	69	100	1235
Like rough hard sex	19	81	100	1233

Table 4. Rape myth acceptance

Variables	*Agree and somewhat agree*	*Disagree and somewhat disagree*	*Total observations*
Stuck-up woman deserve a lesson	7%	93%	1200 = 100%
Women hitchhiking get what they deserve	9%	91%	1203 = 100%
Provocative dress asks for trouble	30%	70%	1223 = 100%
Rape victims have bad reputation	17%	83%	1200 = 100%
Forced sex after necking's woman fault	16%	84%	1197 = 100%
Going to home implies willing to have sex	23%	77%	1218 = 100%

relationships with women. Some of the men said that they had the time, energy, or interest also to engage in a conventional relationship with a woman.

Given the scope of the study our data comes from, we also include the analysis of the relationship between sex work and violence by exploring the 'rape myth acceptance',[19] which implicitly demonstrates a tendency of violence against women (Burt, 1980). The response rates presented in Table 4 indicates that the arrested clients do show some attitudes that validate the 'rape myth acceptance'. Thirty per cent of clients think that provocative dress asks for trouble; 17 per cent think that rape victims have a bad reputation. Twenty-three per cent think that going home with a man implies willingness to have sex with him.

3.1.2 Modelling demand and risk aversion

In what follows, we move to our empirical model of the demand for paid sex, for which we use two specifications: an ordered logit model of demand for paid sex, and a multinomial logit model of the probability of being a regular client.

The first specification is an ordered logit model with four categories of having sex with a sex worker. Let y_n^* be person n's demand for having sex with a sex worker during a year. Here this demand is considered as a latent variable. Let x_n be a vector of explanatory variables that affect demand. β is a vector of unknown coefficients.

Moreover let ϵ_n be a random variable. We then have the following demand function for paid sex:

$$y_n^* = x_n\beta + \varepsilon_n;\ n = 1, 2, \ldots, N. \tag{25}$$

Let y_{nj} be the observation of how many times the clients have had sex with a sex worker during a year, $j = 1, 2, 3, 4$, where $j = 1$ means that the client has not been with a sex worker before he was observed and arrested, $j = 2$ means that the client has been with a sex worker once before, $j = 3$ mean that he has had sex with a sex worker more than once, but less than once per month, and $j = 4$ if the client has had sex with a sex worker more than once per month. Thus, the ordered structure of demand is given by:

$$y_{nj} = \left.\begin{array}{ll} 1 & \text{if client } n \text{ belongs to category } j;\ j = 1, 2, 3, 4 \\ 0 & \text{otherwise.} \end{array}\right\} \tag{26}$$

Let α_j denote the threshold in the ordering of the demand, we then have:

$$\left.\begin{array}{lll} y_{n1} = 1 & \text{if} & y_n^* \le \alpha_1 \\ y_{n2} = 1 & \text{if} & \alpha_1 < y_n^* \le \alpha_2 \\ y_{n3} = 1 & \text{if} & \alpha_2 < y_n^* \le \alpha_3 \\ y_{n4} = 1 & \text{if} & \alpha_3 < y_n^* \end{array}\right\} \tag{27}$$

The thresholds α_j must satisfy $\alpha_1 < \alpha_2 < \alpha_3$. From equations (25) and (27) we obtain:

$$P(y_{nj} = 1) = P(\alpha_{j-1} < y_n^* \le \alpha_j) = P(\alpha_{j-1} - x_n\beta < \varepsilon_n \le \alpha_j - x_n\beta) \tag{28}$$

We will assume that ϵ_n is i.i.d. with c.d.f. $P(\epsilon_n \le u) = F(u)$. The ϵ_n's are assumed to be logistic distributed, with the first moment of the distribution equal to zero and the second moment equal to $\pi^2/3$. Thus:

$$F(u) = \frac{1}{1 + \mathrm{e}^{-u}}. \tag{29}$$

Now we can rewrite equation (28) to yield:

$$P(y_{nj} = 1) = F(\alpha_j - x_n\beta) - F(\alpha_{j-1} - x_n\beta) \tag{30}$$

and where the distribution function $F(.)$ is given in equation (29). Note that:

$$\sum_{j=1}^{4}[P(y_{nj}=1)]=1 \quad \text{so that} \quad P(y_{n4}=1)=1-F(\alpha_3-x_n\beta).$$

The likelihood function is:

$$L(\alpha,\beta)=\prod_{n=1}^{N}\prod_{j=1}^{4}\left[F(\alpha_j-x_n\beta)-F(\alpha_{j-1}-x_n\beta)\right]^{y_{nj}}. \tag{31}$$

The coefficient vectors can then be estimated by maximizing this likelihood (or rather the log likelihood). In order to calculate the marginal effects, we note that from equation (30) we obtain:

$$\frac{\partial P(y_{nj}=1)}{\partial x_n}=\left[\frac{\partial F(\alpha_{j-1}-x_n\beta)}{\partial x_n}-\frac{\partial F(\alpha_j-x_n\beta)}{\partial x_n}\right]\beta \quad \text{for } j=1,2,3,4. \tag{32}$$

From equations (29) and (32) we then derive:

$$\left.\begin{aligned}
\frac{\partial P(y_{n1}=1)}{\partial x_n}&=-F(\alpha_1-x_n\beta)[1-F(\alpha_1-x_n\beta)]\beta\\
\frac{\partial P(y_{n2}=1)}{\partial x_n}&=\{F(\alpha_1-x_n\beta)[1-F(\alpha_1-x_n\beta)]\\
&\quad-F(\alpha_2-x_n\beta)[1-F(\alpha_2-x_n\beta)]\}\beta\\
\frac{\partial P(y_{n3}=1)}{\partial x_n}&=\{F(\alpha_2-x_n\beta)[1-F(\alpha_2-x_n\beta)]\\
&\quad-F(\alpha_3-x_n\beta)[1-F(\alpha_3-x_n\beta)]\}\beta\\
\frac{\partial P(y_{n4}=1)}{\partial x_n}&=\{F(\alpha_3-x_n\beta)[1-F(\alpha_3-x_n\beta)]\}\beta.
\end{aligned}\right\} \tag{33}$$

We note that the first and last marginal effects have an opposite sign. The terms in braces can be positive or negative.

In the second specification of demand we model the probability of being a 'regular' client (multinomial logit). Let U_{nj} be the utility for client n of being j-type of client. When $j=1$, the client is a 'regular' client and when $j=0$ he is an 'experimenter'. We will assume that U_{nj} is given by:

$$U_{nj} = x_n\gamma_j + \varepsilon_{nj}; \quad j=0,1; \quad n=1,2,\ldots,N. \tag{34}$$

The vector x_n is the same as in the ordered logit presented above, expect that it includes 1 to allow for a constant, and γ_j is a vector of alternative specific coefficients. By assuming that ϵ_{nj} is extreme value distributed (the double exponential distribution) with zero expectation and a constant variance, and by assuming utility maximization, we get the following probability for being a 'regular' customer:

$$P(U_{n1} \geq U_{n0}) = \frac{\exp\left(\sum\limits_{k=0}^{K} \gamma_{1k} x_{nk}\right)}{\exp\left(\sum\limits_{k=0}^{K} \gamma_{0k} x_{nk}\right) + \exp\left(\sum\limits_{k=0}^{K} \gamma_{1k} x_{nk}\right)}$$

$$= \frac{\exp\left(\sum\limits_{k=0}^{K} \gamma_k x_{nk}\right)}{1 + \exp\left(\sum\limits_{k=0}^{K} \gamma_k x_{nk}\right)} \tag{35}$$

where $\gamma_k = \gamma_{1k} - \gamma_{0k}$, and $x_{n0} = 1$.

Let $y_{n1} = 1$ if the individual has chosen to be a regular customer, and equal to zero otherwise, and let $\varphi_{n1}(\Sigma_k \gamma_k x_{nk})$ be the choice probability in equation (33). Then the likelihood of the data is:

$$L(\gamma) = \prod_{n=1}^{N} \left[\varphi_{n1}\left(\sum_{k=0}^{K} \gamma_k x_n\right)\right]^{y_{n1}} \left[1 - \varphi_{n1}\left(\sum_{k=0}^{K} \gamma_k x_n\right)\right]^{1-y_{n1}} \tag{36}$$

The coefficients $\gamma_k, k = 0, 1, \ldots, K$ are estimated by maximizing this likelihood (or rather the log-likelihood).

Apart from the demand for paid sex we also estimate the demand for condom use in order to analyse the peculiarity of clients' behaviour with respect to risk. Condom use is almost always negotiated directly between the interested client and the sex worker. Therefore, the client who requires the use of condoms, signals that he has a more risk adverse attitude. The choice probability of using a condom follows from a similar utility maximizing procedure, with an additive random utility model, as the one that led to the likelihood in equation (36).

3.1.3 Empirical estimates

In order to estimate the model for demand of paid sex we would need prices and income variables. In our data we do not observe the price paid, neither do we observe income. What we observe are the following variables: full-time work or not, education (college/or more, or less), age, job-type (executive/business manager versus lower level), race (non-white versus white), married or not. Full-time jobs, education, age, job-type and race are important determinants for income. Income tends to be higher for workers with a full-time job, for workers with higher education, for executive managers and for whites. Moreover, with seniority wage structures income tends also to increase with age. However, education, job-type and race may also have a direct impact on the capacity for reputation losses so that this capacity is lower, i.e., easier to ruin one's reputation, the higher the education is, the more leading job a person has, married versus non-married. Thus, and according to the model in Part I of this book, we would expect full-time work to have a positive impact on demand for paid sex (positive income effect) while the impact of education, age, job type and race are ambiguous.

The data also contains a large number of attitudinal variables. To see whether it was possible to reduce the number of variables, we performed a factor analysis with the purpose of uncovering a possible latent structure of these variables in the data set.[20] These factors will then be included in the demand function. In the factor analysis we exclude those variables which have a percentage of missing values exceeding 22 per cent, as well as missing demographic variables. We derived six factors (as the number of eigenvalues exceeding 1 is 6) which are presented in Table 5.

The first factor, 'against gender violence' is a predictor of violent sexuality. It might indicate that one of the motivations when clients approach the sex workers is the attraction to violence, which can be satisfied through buying sex with sex workers, if found to be a significant factor in explaining demand. The higher the score for this factor, the less gender violent is the client.

The second factor named 'against sex work' can be taken to indicate both relatively conservative views and, alternatively, a commodified perspective towards sex work. The higher the score on this factor, the more the client is against sex work.

The third factor is 'sex workers are not different and dislike their job'. This factor contains also the idea that sex workers are different to other women in that they like men and sex more, and they like sex rougher;

Table 5. The results of the factor analysis

Factors	*Eigenvalues*	*Variables*
Factor 1	0.5305	Forced sex after necking is woman's fault
'Against gender	0.5462	Women hitchhiking deserve rape
violence'	0.5814	Stuck-up women deserve a lesson
	0.6778	Sex fun if woman fights
	0.5036	Some women like being smacked
	0.6396	Want sex more when angry
Factor 2	−0.6296	Prostitution creates problems
'Against sex work'	−0.6586	Cops should crack down on prostitution
	0.7296	Prostitution not wrong
	0.6644	Should legalise prostitution
	0.5323	Should decriminalise prostitution
Factor 3	0.5301	Sex workers like sex more
'Sex workers are	0.4821	Sex workers like sex rougher
not different and	0.5765	Sex workers enjoy work
dislike their jobs'	0.5483	Sex workers like men
	0.4988	Prefer prostitution to relationship
Factor 4 *'Like relationship'*	0.7108	No time for relationship
	0.6952	Don't want relationship responsibilities
	0.4599	Excited by approaching sex workers
Factor 5 *'Variety dislike'*	0.5134	Like to have a variety of partners
	0.4755	Like woman who gets nasty
Factor 6	0.4833	Serious trouble with partner
'Relationship	0.7355	Separated from partner
troubles'	0.6250	Broke up with partner

it can also be used as an indicator for justifying sex commodification and avoids the intrinsic feeling of treatment of sex as a commodity. The higher this factor score, the less clients think that sex workers are different and like their job.

The fourth factor 'like relationships' captures the fact that some respondents prefer sex work to relationships and find the latter burdensome, so they interact with individuals who can respond to their needs without demanding intimate relationships. The higher this factor, the more the clients like relationships and related responsibilities.

Factor five, 'variety dislike', captures the view that sex work forms part of sex consumption, and can, for example, serve to satisfy those sexual appetites that the regular partner is unwilling to satisfy,[21] or the desire for variety of sexual partners. The higher this factor, the less the clients like variety.

Table 6. Effects of variables on demand for sex work

Effects of variables on demand for sex work	*Signs: A priori expectations*	*Signs: Estimates*
Education	?	Not significant
Full time job	+	+
Race	?	+
Executive officer	?	Not significant
Married	?	–
Like relationship	–	–
Dislike variety	–	–
Relationship trouble	+	?
Against sex work	–	–
Dislike control	?	+
Against gender violence	?	+
Sex workers dislike their jobs	?	+

The sixth factor 'relationship troubles' reflects the actual relationship status of respondents. The higher the factor, the less intact and more troubled is the relationship life of the client.

The characteristic of being against sex work may be related to individuals with a lot to lose reputation wise when having commercial sex. Married persons tend to like relationship and may/or may not have troubles with relationship. The latter can also imply that to have sex one has to go outside marriage. These variables, and perhaps dislike variety, may thus capture the impact regular sex may have on the demand for commercial sex. In Table 6, we summarise what our expectations are with respect to how the observed variables and the factors affect demand for sex work.

3.1.4 Results

We use the frequency of encounters with a sex worker during last year as dependent variable in the ordered logit model (see Table A2 in Appendix 1). We consider four categories $j = 1, 2, 3, 4$. Where $j = 1$ means that the client has not been with a sex worker before he was observed and arrested, $j = 2$ means that the client has been with a sex worker once before, $j = 3$ mean that he has had sex with a sex worker more than once, but less than once per month, and $j = 4$ if the client has had sex with a sex worker more than once per month. As far as the probability of being a regular client is concerned, our second model, the dependent variable (see Table A3 in Appendix 1) is defined equal to 1 if the client has been more than once with a sex worker over last year (categories 3 and 4 in the first model). The dependent variable is equal to 0 if the client has been only once or never with a sex worker (categories 1 and 2 in the first model). Using a condom (see Table A3 in Appendix 1) is defined as 1 if the client uses a condom more than once or often, and as 0 if the client never or seldom uses a condom.

The vector x_n of explanatory variables that affect demand in the first model includes the following variables: the six factors defined in the previous paragraph, the working status of the client, his educational level, his age, his occupation, his race, his marital status, a variable about disliking control (see Table A4 for definitions and descriptive statistics). The dataset does not contain information regarding the level of earnings, and hence some of the personal characteristics proxy the income level.

The variable 'dislike control' is defined in Table A5. It takes the value of 1 if clients agree strongly with the statement that they like control during sex. It takes the value of 2 if they agree somehow, value of 3 if they disagree somehow and value equals 4 if they disagree. The higher the value for this variable, the more individuals dislike control.

The vector x_n of explanatory variables for the second and the third model are the same as for the first model but they also include an intercept.

Table 7 contains the estimation results for both the ordered logit for the demand of sex work, the logit for being a regular client and the probability of using a condom.

The ordered logit results imply that demand for paid sex, in terms of frequency per year, is the same across education levels (this variable is not significantly different from 0), it is higher among full-time workers than individuals working less hours (this could be due to an income effect), and non-white individuals demand more than white individuals (this could be an effect related to the particular segment of the sex industry our sample is drawn from, or to the unobserved biases in the sample). Married individuals demand less than non-married. The variable control dislike is very significant and the positive sign implies that the more individuals dislike control, the more they demand sex work; in other words the more they like control, the less they demand. Demand in our sample is increasing with the age of the client. In another specification of the model,[22] we have also added the age when first with a sex worker. We wanted to test the hypothesis that the younger a client starts to visit sex workers, the higher the frequency: a sort of addiction effect. Nevertheless we found that the variable was not significantly different from zero so we rejected the hypothesis of an addiction effect.

Table 7. Estimation results

Variables	*Ordered logit*	*Logit: probability of being a 'regular' client*	*Logit: probability of using condom*
Education = 1 college or more; = 0 otherwise	0.160 (0.194)	0.067 (0.243)	0.067 (0.474)
Work status = 1 full time; = 0 otherwise	0.655** (0.281)	0.656* (0.347)	0.476 (0.564)
Race = 1 if non white; = 0 white	0.491*** (0.186)	0.201 (0.226)	1.121** (0.576)
Job = 1 executives/ business managers; = 0 otherwise	−0.125 (0.170)	−0.151 (0.209)	−0.023 (0.415)
Marriage = 1 married; = 0 otherwise	−0.312* (0.173)	−0.118 (0.213)	0.090 (0.412)
Control dislike	0.276*** (0.096)	0.220* (0.118)	−0.062 (0.234)
Age	0.017* (0.009)	0.030*** (0.011)	−0.031 (0.020)
Factor 1 'against gender violence'	0.181* 0.108*	0.274** 0.136	0.464** 0.259
Factor 2 'against sex work'	−0.159* (0.094)	−0.199* (0.112)	−0.400* (0.222)
Factor 3 'sex workers not different and dislike their job'	0.198** (0.101)	0.200* (0.124)	−0.102 (0.242)
Factor 4 'like relationships'	−0.536*** (0.112)	−0.641*** (0.137)	−0.351 (0.266)
Factor 5 'variety dislike'	−0.968*** (0.121)	−1.031*** (0.151)	0.692*** (0.281)
Factor 6 'relationship troubles'	−0.026 (0.109)	0.006 (0.137)	0.482* (0.293)
Threshold α_1	0.788 (0.550)		
Threshold α_2	2.233*** (0.559)		
Threshold α_3	4.452*** (0.580)		
Constant		−2.501*** (0.692)	3.643*** (1.339)
Number of observations	582	582	570
Mcfaddens rho	0.14	0.18	0.71

Standard errors in parentheses. (Blank: Not significant. ***: Significant at ≤1%, **: Significant at ≤5%, *: Significant at ≤10%).

The positive sign for the coefficient of factor 1 'against gender violence' implies that the higher this variable, i.e., the more the clients dislike violence, the more they demand. In other words, the more clients like gender violence the less they demand. The more clients are against sex work the less they demand (negative sign of factor 2 and significant at 10 per cent). The more they think that sex workers are not different and dislike their job the more they demand (positive sign of factor 3 and significant at 5 per cent). The parameter for factor 4 'like relationships' is negative and strongly significant (1 per cent) and it implies that the more the clients like to be in a relationship with its responsibilities, the less they demand. Factor 5, 'variety dislike', shows that the more they like variety in sex life, the more they demand paid sex (significant at 1 per cent). Factor 6, 'relationship troubles' is not significant.

The results are somewhat mixed compared to prior expectations, but as demonstrated in Table 8, the overall results for the ordered logit in Table 7 shadow for differences in behaviour across individuals with little experience with sex workers (named 'experimenters') and those with more experience (named 'regulars'). In Table 8, we distinguish between four groups of clients. The first two are those who declared to have never had sex with sex workers before or only once before: the 'experimenters' (48 per cent of respondents). Clients in the two last groups are named 'regulars' because they declare having had sex with street sex workers at least more than one time, but less than once a month (third group) or one to three times a month (fourth group), overall these are just over 52 per cent of respondents. Table 8 shows the impact on demand of marginal changes in the explanatory variables, the marginal effects, within each group. As noted above the marginal effects in an ordered logit for the first and the last category must have an opposite sign. The signs for the middle categories are free to vary. In our case, categories 1 and 2 show the same pattern of behaviour and the categories 3 and 4 show the same pattern, but with an opposite sign relative to categories 1 and 2.

The 'experimenters' demand more street sex work the less they work, more if they are white opposed to non-white, more the younger they are and more if they like to have more control when having sex. The 'regulars' characteristics are quite the opposite. The more experimenters are against gender violence the less they demand street sex work (i.e., they demand more, the more gender violent they are). The more experimenters are against sex work, the more they demand; the more they think that the sex workers dislike their job and are not different from other women, the less they demand; the more they like relationships and responsibilities the more they demand, and the less

Table 8. Marginal effects in the ordered logit

Variables	*Never with sex workers*	*Once with sex workers*	*More than 1 time but less then once per month*	*1 to 3 times per month*
Education = 1 college or more; = 0 otherwise	−0.0269 (0.033)	−0.012 (0.014)	0.027 (0.033)	0.012 (0.014)
Work status = 1 Full time; = 0 otherwise	−0.123 (0.059)	−0.033*** (0.008)	0.113** (0.048)	0.0429*** (0.015)
Race = 1 if non white; = 0 white	−0.077*** (0.028)	−0.044** (0.018)	0.079*** (0.029)	0.0425** (0.017)
Job = 1 executives/ business managers = 0 otherwise	0.02 (0.028)	0.01 (0.014)	−0.02 (0.028)	−0.010 (0.013)
Marriage = 1 married; = 0 otherwise	0.051* (0.0287)	0.026* (0.015)	−0.052* (0.029)	−0.025* (0.014)
Control dislike	−0.045*** (0.016)	−0.023*** (0.008)	0.046*** (0.017)	0.022*** (0.008)
Age	−0.002** (0.002)	−0.001* (0.0008)	0.002* (0.0015)	0.001* (0.0007)
Factor 1 'against gender violence'	−0.029* (0.018)	−0.015* (0.0094)	0.030* (0.018)	0.014* (0.0088)
Factor 2 'against sex work'	0.026* (0.015)	0.013* (0.0083)	−0.026* (0.015)	−0.012* (0.0077)
Factor 3 'sex workers not different and dislike their job'	−0.032** (0.016)	−0.016* (0.009)	0.033** (0.0172)	0.016* (0.0083)
Factor 4 'like Relationships'	0.088*** (0.0186)	0.045*** (0.011)	−0.09*** (0.020)	−0.043*** (0.009)
Factor 5 'variety dislike'	0.159*** (0.02)	0.085*** (0.015)	−0.162*** (0.024)	−0.078*** (0.012)
Factor 6 'relationship troubles'	0.004 (0.017)	0.002 (0.009)	−0.004 (0.018)	−0.002 (0.008)

Standard errors in brackets. (Blank: non significant, *: significant at 10%, **: 5%, ***: 1%).

they like variety in their sex life, the more they demand. For the regulars all of these effects are reversed.

Thus the experimenters correspond to a more machist type, with negative views of women, of sex work and of sex workers (who are believed to be different from other women but condemned at the same time), and viewing street sex work as a complement to stable relationships. The regulars have more liberal views of women, of sex work and of sex workers, the more they dislike control the more they demand, and they like variety. Their demand also increases with age and with having a permanent job, which may indicate a positive income effect. These appear to be men who are happy to satisfy their sexual wants through sex work, which they prefer to relationships. In Table 7 we also give the estimates of the probability of being a 'regular' client as opposed to being an 'experimenter'. Comparing these results with the marginal effects for the 'regulars' derived from the ordered logit given in Table 7, we observe that the results are quite similar, which is a further confirmation of the conclusions drawn above.

In Table 7 we also report the estimates from the use of condoms, which is a measure of risk aversion on the part of the client (Gertler *et al.*, 2003). Concentrating on the significant parameters[23] we note that the probability of using a condom is higher among the non-white compared to the white respondents. The probability of using a condom is higher among those who are opposed to gender violence relative to those who are not, and the probability of using a condom is higher the more they favour sex work and the less they like variety. It is also interesting to note that among those with a good relationship the probability of using a condom is lower than among those with a broken relationship. Thus the users of condoms seem to fit the profile of the regulars, whereas the non-users fit that of the experimenters.

The results of our empirical analysis confirm the behavioural assumptions behind our theoretical framework: stigmatisation of clients and sex workers are important characteristics of this market (as reflected in the attitudes of clients in the sample towards sex work, towards sex workers and towards being caught), and demand for paid sex is not simply a substitute for demand for free sex. Both of these general results confirm the findings of the empirical literature discussed in Part I.

Moreover, in our sample there appear to be two distinct groups of clients, whose personal characteristics and attitudes are radically opposite: experimenters, to whom street sex work is a complement to stable relationships, and who hold negative views of women, of sex work and of sex workers; and regulars, who hold more liberal views, like variety and find relationships a burden, and for whom paid sex is a commodity and a normal good whose demand increases with income. The experimenters demand more sex the more they like to have control while the regulars do the opposite. This suggests the need to explicitly incorporate this variable when modelling demand for sex work, and also to further test with empirical evidence whether control in sex is related to perception of control in other areas of a clients' life. This seems particularly important in order to understand whether it is possible to test empirically the idea put forward in several papers that demand for sex work is related to the construction of male identity (Marttila, 2003; Garofalo, 2002). In this sense, it would also be interesting to see which factors are at play in women's demand for male sex work services.

As far as attitudes towards risk are concerned, we note that risk aversion is also correlated to our two clients' profiles, with experimenters being more risk loving and regulars more risk averse. Notwithstanding the selection bias problems presented by our data, our results appear to be in line with those of other studies. Furthermore, our evidence also confirms that the demand for sex work is a phenomenon with multifaceted characteristics which need to be properly investigated and understood when designing regulation for this sector. This is particularly relevant since regulation is overwhelmingly concerned with supply-side considerations, and failure to understand the demand side of this phenomenon is likely to generate ineffective policy outcomes.

3.2 A specific segment of the supply side

Sexually exploited trafficked women

Our research on the supply side of the market is confined here to a specific segment of the market: trafficked women. We want to underline at the beginning of this chapter that this segment is only a part of the supply side of the market. Most individuals enter the sex market freely and they are not included in the following analysis. As we stressed in Part II, the decision to enter this labour market depends on feasible alternatives, their wages and stigma/reputation considerations. Our first intention was to analyse the choices of individuals who entered the market freely. Nevertheless, despite many attempts, we were not able to find a data set with information about sex workers. The analysis of sexually exploited trafficked women is therefore driven by the data. In fact, the increasing political attention to the crime of trafficking has allowed the International Organisation for Migration to collect data on trafficked individuals, and among those, the sexually exploited ones.

3.2.1 Definition of trafficking and exploitation

Trafficking in women has been estimated to generate US$12 billion a year, enough to be ranked just after trafficking in weapons and drugs (Bindel, 2003; see also the recent UNODC report: UNODC, 2006). Within economics, theoretical or empirical research on trafficking in human beings – its actors, market and institutional characteristics – is thin or non-existent, and lack of suitable data is a credible if not entirely genuine excuse.

This section addresses this gap by analysing working and living conditions of individuals that have reported to the Anti-Trafficking Unit of the International Organization for Migration (IOM henceforth) for assistance and have been identified as 'victims of trafficking' for the purpose of 'sexual exploitation'. The IOM has developed a Counter-Trafficking Module Database to collect information on victims of trafficking.[24] This database enables IOM to reconstruct the trafficking scenario by analysing the situation of the victims before and during the exploitation. It also allows the IOM to better target the assistance programmes and reintegration of the victims. Our analysis here is confined to the sub-sample identified as female victims of sexual exploitation.

Although the subject matter of the research is seemingly neat, 'victims', 'trafficking' and 'sexual exploitation' are loaded terms over which there is no clear consensus in the literature. Contested semantics invariably signals differences in theoretical and policy perspectives, whereby the same word hides different contours for the phenomenon under investigation as well as a different research and policy agenda.

According to the Palermo Protocol signed by 80 countries in December 2000 after two years of negotiation:[25]

> 'Trafficking in persons' shall mean the recruitment, transportation, transfer, harbouring, or receipt of persons, by means of the threat or use of force or other forms of coercion, of abduction, of fraud, of deception, of the abuse of power or of a position of vulnerability, or of the giving or receiving of payments or benefits to achieve the consent of a person having control over another person, for the purpose of exploitation. Exploitation shall include, at a minimum, the exploitation of the prostitution of others or other forms of sexual exploitation, forced labour or services, slavery or practices similar to slavery, servitude or the removal of organs.
>
> (Article. 3a, United Nations, 2000)

> The consent of a victim of trafficking in persons to the intended exploitation shall be irrelevant where any of the means set forth in article 3a have been used.
>
> (Article. 3b, United Nations, 2000)

Many would agree that identifying those who have been trafficked is less problematic now thanks to this protocol. But while the definition agreed upon is found useful by opposite sides in the debate (Gallagher, 2001), several issues remain unresolved. One such issue is whether sexual services should be recognised as labour services. In the effort to overcome the deep political division between those for whom prostitution cannot be entered out of truly free choice because it always violates the human right to dignity and those who emphasise agency on the part of prostitutes and advocate full labour rights, Article 3b of the Protocol qualifies as 'victims' also those migrants that may have consented to prostitution in the first place, provided they were subjected to exploitative conditions at some point. At the same time, the Protocol gives each country the choice of whether or not prostitution should be considered as work and granted commensurate rights.

The consensus achieved by the Protocol on the irrelevance of the initial consent needs to be emphasised. Take the example of somebody agreeing to do sex work in a night club for a given wage and number of hours and under conditions of freedom of movement. If this initial agreement actually lead to a job where s/he does not have a choice over clients, money or contraception and is not free to move, then the Protocol applies.[26] In other words, the consent of a victim of trafficking in persons to the intended exploitation is irrelevant where any of the 'means' identified in the Protocol's definition of trafficking have been used. Indeed, in many human trafficking cases, there is initial consent or cooperation between victims and traffickers. This is followed by more coercive, abusive and exploitative actions on the part of traffickers (UNODC, 2006).

One additional issue is what exactly constitutes sexual exploitation. Given that the Protocol does not settle the question of whether prostitution should be treated as work, it is hardly surprising that what constitutes sexual exploitation is also left undefined. GAATW (2001: 31) reports that no agreement could be reached during the negotiations on the term 'exploitation of the prostitution of others or other forms of exploitation'. Nor could expressions like 'abuse of power' or 'other forms of coercion' be further elaborated upon (O'Connell Davidson and Andersen, 2006).

While the above issues are of general interest to any analysis of trafficking for sexual exploitation, the specific terms of the debate surrounding the Protocol are not central to the kind of analysis we pursue in this book. For this reason we shall hereafter use the terms sexually exploited victims of trafficked or trafficking sex workers interchangeably.

3.2.2 Description of the IOM data set

Data in the IOM dataset are collected from IOM field missions based on two standardised questionnaires. The first questionnaire is administered to all individuals applying for assistance and is used for screening. Applicants admitted to the assistance programme are administered the final questionnaire which includes all the questions from the screening questionnaire plus additional information. Information concerns demographic characteristics, socio-economic and family background, recruitment and trafficking process, type of exploitation in the destination country, work and pay conditions while trafficked, and current health conditions. We chose the data set provided by the assistance interviews because the screening interviews did not provide enough information about personal characteristics of the victims.

The data set has two main limitations. The first one is the selection of the individuals in the sample. Because data comes from IOM field missions, it is not a representative sample of the population of trafficked individuals. Individuals come from the countries where the IOM missions were located. Moreover, individuals in the programme may have on average different characteristics from the individuals who did not enter into the IOM programme; one obvious example of this possible bias is the high level of education of women (6 per cent have a university degree). More educated women could find it easier to report the traffickers relative to the less educated. The second major problem with the data is the frequency of missing values that reaches 50 per cent or above for some 'sensitive' questions.

The complete data set include individuals who were trafficked for sexual exploitation (86 per cent), for forced labor (11 per cent), and other forms of exploitation (3 per cent); of the sexually exploited individuals, 89 per cent are women and 11 per cent men (see Table 9). In our analysis we select the sub-sample of sexually exploited women. The reason for this choice relies on the large number of missing variables for males.[27]

The majority of IOM assisted victims had been trafficked for sexual exploitation out of their own country,[28] originating from ex-Soviet Union, Eastern and Balkan countries and have been found working in one of the following destinations: Italy, Greece, Spain, Portugal, Lebanon, Israel, Turkey, Syria, Albania, Bosnia, Romania, Bulgaria, Croatia, Macedonia, Moldavia, Serbia & Montenegro, Slovenia, Armenia, Georgia, Kazakhstan, Kyrgyzstan, Russia, Tajikistan,

Table 9. Trafficked individuals by gender and type of exploitation in the IOM data set

	Female	%	*Male*	%	*Total*	%
Forced labour	430	8.4	230	27.9	660	11.1
Sexual services	4559	89.0	560	68.0	5119	86.2
Other	128	2.5	33	4.0	161	2.7
Total	5117	100	823	100	5940	100

Note: Total percentage values may not equal 100 per cent due to rounding of numbers.

Table 10. Sexually exploited trafficked women: personal characteristics (total number of observations 4559)

Trafficking	Internal	27.3%
	International	72.7%
	Total	4211
Age	Less than 9	0.1%
	> 9&≤20	37.0%
	> 20&≤30	54.4%
	> 30&≤40	7.4%
	> 40	1.1%
	Total	4533
Marital status	Cohabiting/married	13.2%
	Divorced	11.4%
	Single	68.5%
	Other	6.9%
	Total	3368
Children	No	65.8%
	Yes	34.2%
	Total	3472
Education	College/university	5.9%
	High school	24.6%
	Middle/trade school	30.0%
	Primary school	17.5%
	Other	20.1%
	None	2.0%
	Total	3312

Note: The number of observations for each variable changes because of the exclusion of missing values. Total percentage values may not equal 100 per cent due to rounding of numbers.

Turkmenistan, Uzbekistan, Lithuania, Iran, Azerbaijan, Belarus, Ukraine (see Appendix 2 for details).

Table 10 shows the personal characteristics of the victims. 54 per cent of the women are between 20 and 30 years old. A surprising large number had children (34 per cent), more than expected on the basis of marriage status: only 25 per cent reported being a partner in a relation, married or divorced. The educational level is not low. Although the majority of victims had not gone beyond middle/trade school, a non-negligible 25 per cent had completed high school and 6 per cent had received college/university education.

Table 11 reports the economic status of the family and own occupational status prior to being trafficked: 59 per cent of trafficked female sex workers declared to come from a poor family, despite the fact that the vast majority of participants were employed prior

Table 11. Sexually exploited trafficked women: economic profile

Family economic status	Poor	59.1%
	Standard	20.1%
	Very poor	20.5%
	Well of	0.2%
	Total	2857
Occupation at home	Agriculture	1.6%
	Domestic	2.8%
	Industry	4.0%
	Private/public	78.6%
	Self-employment	5.3%
	Sex industry	1.2%
	Other	6.5%
	Total	1765
Previous salary	Monthy/US$	51.5
	Total	1305
Amount sold	US$ total	4659
	Total	721

Note: The number of observations for each variable changes because of the exclusion of missing values. Total percentage values may not equal 100 per cent due to rounding of numbers.

to departure. However, the average level of declared monthly earnings did not exceed US$52 per month, which is in sharp contrast to the average amount of money for which they were sold, i.e., US$4659. Both these figures must be taken with great caution, given that not all answered either questions.

Table 12 describes the recruitment and the trafficking process. The vast majority of them had been recruited via personal contacts (84 per cent) while television or Internet advertisements accounted for an additional 7 per cent. Five per cent were kidnapped and less than 1 per cent had been sold by family members. In most of the cases, the recruiters offered the victims the opportunity to find a job abroad in the hope to attract them. More than half of the recruiters were strangers (53 per cent of valid answers) whereas friends made up more than a quarter (29 per cent). The gender composition of the recruiters was fairly balanced with 46 per cent females and 50 per cent were males (with 4 per cent not identified gender). The typical work being offered was domestic help/babysitter (28 per cent), followed by selling/waitress/sweatshops (24 per cent) and with dancer. A non-negligible share declared being explicitly offered sex work (9 per cent).

Table 12. Sexually exploited trafficked women: recruitment characteristics

How recruited?	Kidnapped	5.4%
	Internet/newspaper/TV	7.4%
	Sold by family	0.5%
	Personal	84.1%
	Other	2.5%
	Total	3103
Gender of the recruiter	Both	4.4%
	Female	45.6%
	Male	50.0%
	Total	3361
What was offered (answers here include kidnapped people)	Job	84.7%
	Marriage	1.7%
	Study	0.1%
	Tourism	6.2%
	Other	7.4%
	Total	3497
Type of job offered	Agriculture	2.1%
	Domestic help/babysitter	28.0%
	Dancer	23.8%
	Sex worker	8.5%
	Selling/sweatshop/waitress	24.6%
	Other/begging	13.0%
	Total	1733
Relationship with the recruiter	Business	0.5%
	Partner	2.7%
	Family/relative	3.3%
	Friend	29.3%
	Stranger	53.1%
	Pimp	0.7%
	Other	10.3%
	Total	3018
Knew were sold	No	42.7%
	Yes	57.3%
	Total	2633
Victim of trafficking before this occasion	No	90.7%
	Yes	9.3%
	Total	1857
How was freed	Client	5.3%
	Family	1.3%
	Friend	0.9%
	Law enforcement	26.0%
	NGO	29.5%
	Self	31.2%
	Other	5.9%
	Total	3332

Note: The number of observations for each variable changes because of the exclusion of missing values. Total percentage values may not equal 100 per cent due to rounding of numbers.

A small but non-negligible group of victims had been trafficked more than once (9 per cent).

Table 13 describes some characteristics, attitudes and conditions of trafficked sex workers and their clients. Most sex workers reported civilian and local clients as opposed to police, military or international, although the reported incidence of the latter is not negligible. Almost half of them worked in bars and nightclubs (48 per cent), 12 per cent worked in the streets, 11 per cent worked in private houses and apartments, 7 per cent in sauna or massage parlours; only a small share (4 per cent) was employed by call-girl and escort agencies.

The majority of victims, often the vast majority of them, reported being denied basic working rights (Table 13). The overwhelming majority was denied any freedom of choice over clients (96 per cent) or over sexual services (88 per cent). Furthermore, more than half were allowed to use condoms regularly, the remaining half being entirely or partially denied this option (9 and 40 per cent, respectively).

Table 14 provides information about sexual exploitation in the destination country. Freedom of movement was granted to a tiny minority (6 per cent) , while the vast majority had none (58 per cent) or could move only if accompanied (36 per cent). More than 82 per cent of trafficked sex workers had been abused, the most frequent types of abuse being, in order of importance, denial of food and medical care (35 per cent), physical assault (31 per cent), and sexual assault/rape (17 per cent). The percentage of clients being abusive is not negligible since 11 per cent of the abusers belonged to the category 'clients'. At the same time, 5 per cent of the clients actively contributed to free the sexually exploited victims (see Table 12). However, most participants had freed themselves by escaping and soliciting assistance from the authorities (31 per cent) or thanks to the intervention of NGOs (29 per cent) and law enforcement agents (26 per cent).

The reported working schedule also depicts an alarming picture. Table 15 shows that trafficked sex workers worked on average 7 days per week and 13 hours per day, serving on average five clients per day. Customers were charged US$94 on average, with only 10 per cent of them being asked to pay more than US$150. However, fees were reported by only 235 interviewees.

In Di Tommaso *et al.* (2007) we use the theoretical framework of the capability approach to conceptualise well-being deprivation and we estimate a MIMIC (Multiple Indicators Multiple Causes) model on the data described above. Well being is an intrinsically unobservable variable of which we can only observe some indicators that are measured with errors. These indicators measure abuse, freedom of

Table 13. Sexually exploited trafficked women: characteristics of the job

Clients	
Mainly internationals	7.9
Mainly locals	73.5
Other	18.6
Total	1605 = 100.00
Occupation of clients	
Civilians	55.2
Military	4.2
Other	31.9
Police	8.7
Total	620 = 100.00
Type of working location	
Bars/Nightclubs	47.9
Escort/Call-girl agencies	3.6
Hotels	2.4
Motels	3.2
Other	12.9
Private houses/Apartments	10.8
Sauna/Massage parlours	7.2
Streets	11.9
Total	2499 = 100.00
Allowed to use condoms?	
At all times	5.6
Never	8.5
Not regularly	39.9
Regularly	46.0
Total	2250 = 100.00
Freedom of choice, over client?	
None	96.3
Partial	3.0
Yes	0.6
Total	627 = 100.00
Freedom of choice, over sex services?	
None	88.0
Partial	6.2
Yes	5.7
Total	609 = 100.00

Note: The number of observations for each variable changes because of the exclusion of missing values. Total percentage values may not equal 100 per cent due to rounding of numbers.

Table 14. Sexually exploited trafficked women: deprivation of the victims

Medical care	Denied	58.1%
	Occasional	18.0%
	Only in emergency cases	16.2%
	Regular	7.7%
	Total	2408
Abuse	No	17.9%
	Yes	82.1%
	Total	3059
By whom abused	Clients	10.7%
	Pimp	20.8%
	Supervisor	24.1%
	Other	44.3%
	Total	2264
Nature of abuse	Physical assault	3.1%
	Psychological abuse	8.5%
	Sexual assault/rape	17.4%
	Threats	6.5%
	Other/denial of med. care, food	35.5%
	Total	1644
Freedom of movement	No restrictions	6.4%
	Only accompanied	35.8%
	Totally denied	57.8%
	Total	3014

Note: The number of observations for each variable changes because of the exclusion of missing values. Total percentage values may not equal 100 per cent due to rounding of numbers.

Table 15. Sexually exploited trafficked women: monetary terms of the exploitation

	Obs	*Mean*	*Std. Dev.*	*Min*	*Max*
Number of customers/day	1521	5.157	4.68	1	40
Average charge per client (US$)	2.35	94.31	116.27	0.02	1000
Amount allowed to keep per day	72	78.60	162.15	0.25	1000
Days worked per week	830	6.88	0.65	1	7
Hours worked per day	632	13.11	4.99	1	24

The number of observations for each variable changes because of the exclusion of missing values.

movement and access to medical care. This model also allows us to estimate the effects of some covariants on this measure of well being. We find that all the indicators we use are important to measure well being, access to medical care having the highest loading. Working in apartments or in secluded spaces has a negative effect on well being relative to working on the street. Having a previous working experience and coming from a relatively well off family have a positive effect on well being of trafficked women. The effect of education is negative. Our interpretation is that women with higher education are more profitable to the traffickers relative to uneducated women. As a consequence their freedom of movement is more constrained compared to the uneducated, less 'valuable' women. We find support for this interpretation because education has a strong positive effect on charge per client.

Conclusions

Our aim with this book is to encourage rigorous analysis of a neglected area of economic activity, which shares some features with other areas of primarily female employment and of the informal sector, and is further burdened by the wide stigmatisation suffered by those who work in it which affects their security, social standing and availability of alternative opportunities. Our agenda is, as stated at the outset, both of advancing the conditions of those who work in the industry through a better understanding of its structure, and of enriching both the fields of application and the methodology of analysis currently deployed by economists.

The sex industry is fundamentally characterised by stigma and our model shows that it is possible to endogenise this key feature to describe demand and supply conditions, and determine different market equilibria on the basis of which policy implications can be discussed. We have made no restrictive assumptions regarding pay, and nature of forgone opportunities for the sex worker, and concentrating on income, reputation and personal attitude variables we have determined price and quantities of equilibrium for different submarkets and more importantly produced a framework in which the effect of policy can be simulated. We have also hypothesised a threshold both for clients and sex workers, which has to be crossed in order to demand and supply the first unit of sex. Our contribution hopefully shows that it is possible to use economic tools to describe the impact of policies on the sex industry, by assuming that stigma is a fundamental characteristic of the industry and incorporating the effect of policies on social norms.

Our empirical study has focussed on the determinants of demand and found that, as suggested by other empirical studies, control is indeed a component motivating clients. This suggests the need to explicitly incorporate this variable when modelling demand for sex work, and also to further test with empirical evidence whether control in sex is related to perception of control in other areas of a clients' life. This seems particularly important in order to understand whether it is possible to test empirically the idea put forward in several papers that demand for sex work is related to the construction of male identity (Marttila, 2003; Garofalo, 2002). In this sense, it would also be interesting to see which factors are at play in women's demand for male sex work services, which has been found in other studies to be also characterised by socially constructed differences between clients and sex workers.

Further study is obviously needed to redress the balance of informed public policy for this area, which has largely responded so far to public order, health and morality concerns and rarely focussed on the varied interests and needs of those who supply sexual services, which more often than not are alternatively viewed as victims or villains, and rarely as workers deserving respect. Prostitution policy that makes economic sense will only be possible once such concerns are complemented with rigorous analysis of available empirical evidence, so that alternative regimes and their effect on participants in the market can be assessed, Until then this will remain a denied industry, and denied will be the rights of those who work in it.

Part IV

Appendices

Appendix 1

Table A1. Descriptive statistics of the variables used in the factor analysis. Number of observations = 582

		Agree strongly = 1	*Agree somewhat = 2*	*Disagree somewhat = 3*	*Disagree strongly = 4*	*Total %*
Factor 1	Forced sex after necking is woman's fault	3.26	10.48	23.02	63.23	100
	Women hitchhiking deserve rape	2.23	4.81	14.43	78.52	100
	Stuck-up women deserve a lesson	2.41	3.26	8.25	86.08	100
	Sex fun if woman fights	1.55	4.12	11.68	82.65	100
	Some women like being smacked	3.09	18.38	25.95	52.58	100
	Want sex more when angry	1.72	4.64	9.79	83.85	100
Factor 2	Prostitution creates problems	15.46	25.77	29.55	29.21	100
	Cops should crack down on prostitution	13.06	26.12	26.12	34.71	100
	Prostitution not wrong	17.35	34.02	30.76	17.87	100
	Should legalise prostitution	41.24	33.33	12.03	13.4	100
	Should decriminalise prostitution	39.18	32.47	17.01	11.34	100
Factor 3	Sex workers like sex more	4.3	15.64	34.19	45.88	100
	Sex workers like sex rougher	2.58	15.54	32.99	51.89	100
	Sex workers enjoy work	2.75	22.85	47.77	26.63	100
	Sex workers like men	5.84	34.36	42.44	17.35	100
Factor 4	Prefer prostitution to relationship	6.19	15.98	21.31	56.53	100
	No time for relationship	13.06	22.16	18.21	46.56	100
	Don't want relationship responsibilities	12.71	17.7	17.53	52.06	100
Factor 5	Excited by approaching sex workers	12.89	38.14	24.05	24.91	100
	Like to have a variety of partners	14.78	35.57	19.93	29.73	100
	Like woman who gets nasty	22.68	35.4	19.42	22.51	100
		Yes = 1	*No = 0*	*Total %*	*Total obs*	
Factor 6	Serious trouble with partner	32.99	67.01	100	582	
	Separated from partner	20.79	79.21	100	582	
	Broke up with partner	20.1	97.9	100	582	

Note: Total percentage values may not equal 100 per cent due to rounding of numbers.

Table A2. Dependent variable for the ordered logit

Frequency of sex with sex worker during last year	*No. of Obs 582 Frequency per cent*
= 1 never	25.4
= 2 once	27.0
= 3 more than 1 but less than once per month	35.0
= 4 1 to 3 times per month	12.5

Note: Total percentage values may not equal 100 per cent due to rounding of numbers.

Table A3. (a) Dependent variable for the probability of being a regular client; (b) Dependent variable for the probability of using a condom

(a) Frequency of sex with sex worker during last year	*No. of Obs 582 Frequency per cent*	*(b) Condom Use*	*No. of Obs 570 Frequency per cent*
= 1 if more than once with a sex worker in the last year	52.4	= 1 use condom more than once and often	94.4
= 0 if never or once with a sex worker last year	47.6	= 0 use condom never and seldom	5.6

Table A4. Descriptive statistics of the variables of the sample used for estimation in Table 6. Number of observations = 582

Variable	*Mean*	*St. dev*	*Min*	*Max*
Education := 1 college or more, = 0 otherwise	0.7457	0.435	0	1
Work status = 1 Full time, = 0 otherwise	0.907	0.290	0	1
Race := 1 if non white, = 0 white	0.355	0.4791	0	1
Job := 1 executives/managers, = 0 otherwise	0.4329	0.495	0	1
Marriage := 1 married, = 0 otherwise	0.482	0.500	0	1
Control dislike	2.735	0.941	1	4
Age	39	10.009	18	76
Factor 1 'against gender violence'	0.035	0.8693	−5.488	1.154
Factor 2 'against sex work'	0.011	0.929	−2.264	2.189
Factor 3 'sex workers not different and dislike their job'	0.0006	0.885	−3.0865	2.5491
Factor 4 'like relationships'	0.0077	0.8919	−2.623	1.667
Factor 5 'variety dislike'	−0.020	0.856	−2.424	2.490
Factor 6 'relationship troubles '	0.004	0.834	−1.385	4.129

Table A5. Control like

Do you like control during sex?	*Total observations = 582* *Frequency per cent*
= 1 if agree strongly	10.3
= 2 if agree somewhat	30.1
= 3 if disagree somewhat	35.4
= 4 if disagree strongly	24.2

Appendix 2

Graphs A1 and A2 show, respectively, where trafficked sex workers originating from the Balkans and from ex-Soviet Union countries agreed to work in: more than half the nationals from the Balkans had agreed to work in Mediterranean countries while ex-Russian nationals had agreed to work in the Middle East, their own countries or the Balkans.

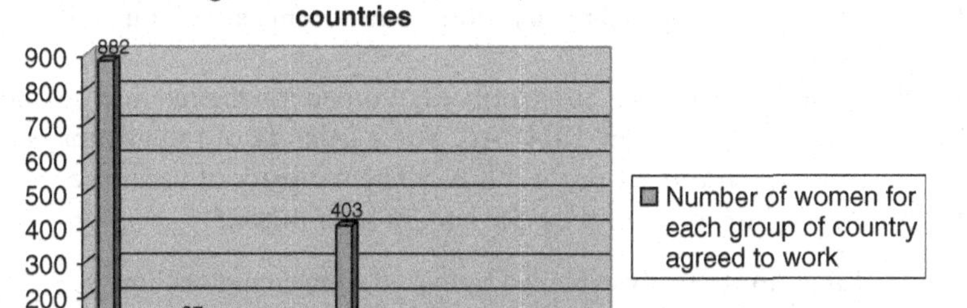

Group 1: Italy, Greece, Spain, Portugal. Group 2: Egypt, Algeria, Marocco. Group 3: Lebanon, Israel, Turkey, Syria. Group 4: Liberia, Chad, Kenya, Benin, Mali, Togo, Ghana, Niger, Uganda, Cote d' Ivoire, Gabon, Guinea. Group 5: Argentina, Ecuador, Columbia, Chile, Paraguay, Peru. Group 6: Bahamas, Dominica, Honduras. Group 7: Albania, Bosnia, Romania, Bulgaria, Croatia, Macedonia, Moldavia, Serbia & Montenegro, Slovenia. Group 8: Czech Rep., Hungary, Poland, Slovakia. Group 9: Germany, Switzerland, Ireland, UK, Belgium, France. Group 10 Armenia, Georgia, Kazakhistan, Kyrgyzstan, Russia, Tajikistan, Turkmenistan, Uzbekistan, Lithuania, Iran, Azebarjan, Belarusia, Ukraine. Group 11: China, Macau. Group 12: Cambodia, Vietnam. Group 13: Maldives, Sri Lanka, Philippines, Indonesia.

Graph A1. Countries agreed to work for: women from Balkans

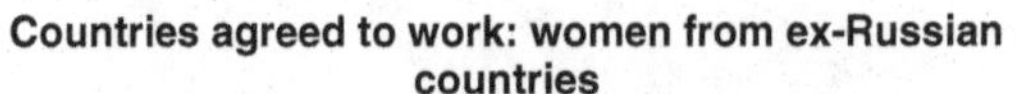

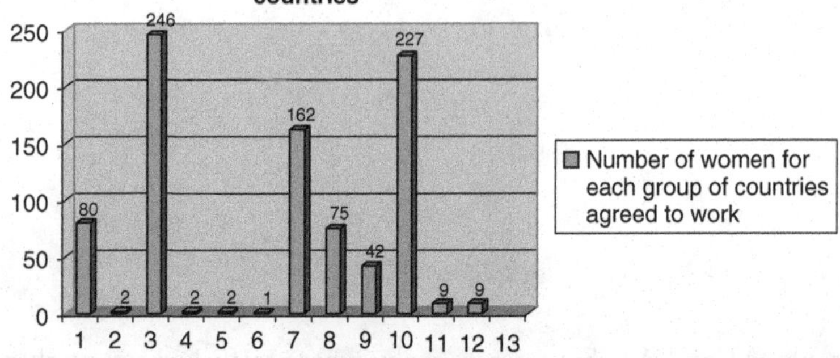

Group 1: Italy, Greece, Spain, Portugal. Group 2: Egypt, Algeria, Marocco. Group 3: Lebanon, Israel, Turkey, Syria. Group 4: Liberia, Chad, Kenya, Benin, Mali, Togo, Ghana, Niger, Uganda, Cote d' Ivoire, Gabon, Guinea. Group 5: Argentina, Ecuador, Columbia, Chile, Paraguay, Peru. Group 6: Bahamas, Dominica, Honduras. Group 7: Albania, Bosnia, Romania, Bulgaria, Croatia, Macedonia, Moldavia, Serbia & Montenegro, Slovenia. Group 8: Czech Rep., Hungary, Poland, Slovakia. Group 9: Germany, Switzerland, Ireland, UK, Belgium, France. Group 10: Armenia, Georgia, Kazakhistan, Kyrgyzstan, Russia, Tajikistan, Turkmenistan, Uzbekistan, Lithuania, Iran, Azebarjan, Belarusia, Ukraine. Group 11: China, Macau. Group 12: Cambodia, Vietnam. Group 13: Maldives, Sri Lanka, Philippines, Indonesia.

Graph A2. Countries agreed to work for: women from ex-Soviet union

The nationality of the subgroup of women trafficked for sexual exploitation is reported in Table A6. For a *legenda* of the groups, see the footnote to Graph A1 or Graph A2. The majority of victims comes from Eastern European and ex-Soviet Union countries.

Table A6. Sexually exploited trafficked women: nationality

Group 1	0	0.0%
Group 2	1	0.0%
Group 3	0	0.0%
Group 4	164	3.6%
Group 5	42	0.9%
Group 6	46	1.0%
Group 7	2751	60.4%
Group 8	7	0.2%
Group 9	1	0.0%
Group 10	1505	33.0%
Group 11	7	0.2%
Group 12	15	0.3%
Group 13	17	0.4%
Total	4556	100.0%

Notes

1 See the seminal work of Fred Hirsch (Hirsch, 1977) and Pagano (1999), widely used among other fields in cooperative and non-cooperative bargaining model of the family.

2 To this extent it is useful to refer to the literature on emotional intelligence (Goleman, 1996). The idea of Emotional Intelligence comes from some discoveries made by neuro-biologists working with brain damaged patients. The most important decisions taken by individuals are not only driven by what is usually called intelligence but also by the first response that our original brain (the part we have in common with primates) sends to our body, usually called 'emotional reaction'.

3 Prostitution contract: 'the client parts with money or other material benefits in order to secure power over the sex worker person which he (or more rarely she) could not otherwise exercise', 'the essence of the contract is that the sex worker agrees not to use her personal desire or erotic interest as the determining criteria for her sexual interaction' (O'Connell Davidson, 2001), 'The rights and wrongs of prostitution', page 4 and page 14) it 'grants one the right to control if and when they have sex, with whom, and how and denies those same rights to another' (*ibid.* page 12).

4 'Taking money for bodily services, but without the option of using their body, in their work, in what Marx would call a "truly human" manner of functioning, by which he meant, among other things, having some choices about the work to be performed, some reasonable measure of control over its condition and outcome, and also the chance to use thought and skill rather than just to function as a cog in a machine' (Nussbaum, *ibid.* page 298).

5 Radin defines commodification as 'the social process by which something comes to be apprehended as a commodity, as well as the state of affairs once the process has taken place' and 'Commodities are socially constructed as objects separate from the self and social relations', so that commodification of personal attributes and relations assumes that 'human attributes are possessions bearing a value that can be characterised in money terms and implies that these possessions can and should be separable from persons to be exchanged through the free market' (p. 6).

6 The sample was taken by distributing a survey to customers of a Sexpo exhibition held in Melbourne 2001. This is a commercial event hosting a wide range of exhibitors of products associated with sex;

of 4905 respondents, 1225 received a version of the questionnaires with questions on sex workers. Among 1225 respondents, 612 were men and 601 were women.

7 Dispatches: Sex on the Street; Channel 4 season Prostitution – The Laws Don't Work, Channel 4, September 2002.

8 Sex refers to the biological differences between males and females, whereas gender refers to the meaning that a culture gives to such biological difference, constructed on the basis of actual or perceived differences between men and women (Harding, 1986; Rubin, 1975). Gender relations are therefore different in different cultures, and they are not given by nature but socially constructed. Social construction refers to the idea that our identities are shaped through the transmission of values into children from birth in the family, education systems, mass-media, etc. These shape our behaviour and values along different dimensions, including class, race, age, and gender. Identity is not determined by biology, but by belonging to the social world, and relative social positioning and power of an actor are likewise socially determined.

9 Sullivan and Simon (1998) find that 17.7 per cent of American males have paid for sex, while Cameron and Collins (2003) find that only 4.9 per cent of UK males have done so.

10 'Prostitution allows certain powers of command over one person's body to be exercised by another' (O'Connell-Davidson, 1998, p. 9).

11 Note that a_1, a_3 and a_4 could depend on observed as well as unobserved individual characteristics such that a high status individual may have a higher a_3 than a lower status individual.

12 $\beta_1, \beta_2, \beta_3$ are all positive. They may depend on individual characteristics.

13 The demand curve starts at $w = a_1 - a_3 + a_4 I_c$ which is below $a_1 - a_3 + a_4 I_c - a_{33} R_c$ because a_{33} is negative.

14 The supply curve starts at $w = b_1 + b_{11} H_p + b_3$ which is higher than $b_1 + b_{11} H_p + b_3 + b_{33} R_p$ because b_{33} is negative.

15 The Inter-university Consortium for Political and Social Research (a unit within the Institute for Social Research at the University of Michigan, USA) provided the data. Data are available and downloadable from: http://www.icpsr.umich.edu:8080/ABSTRACTS/02859.xml?format=ICPSR

16 Though refusals constituted the largest single category of non-completions, language barriers and late arrivals also accounted for a substantial proportion. Of these 1342 respondents, 36 from San Francisco and 15 from Las Vegas completed a Spanish-language version of the questionnaire. Completing the English version of the questionnaire were 950 men from San Francisco, 254 from Las Vegas, 77 from Portland, and 10 from Santa Clara.

17 The nationally representative sample data of The National Health and Social Life Survey are provided by Monto (2000b). The survey data are collected by personal interviews and self-administered questionnaires, and provide information on the sexual experiences as well as social, demographic (race, education, political and religious affiliation and occupation), attitudinal (amongst which attitudes towards premarital sex, the appeal of particular sexual practices, levels of satisfaction with particular sexual relationships), and health-related characteristics. The overall response rate was 78.6 per cent of the 4369 eligible respondents

selected for inclusion in the study. The sample reported in Table 1 includes only the non-missing values.

18 Because men in the sample were almost all arrested while propositioning a decoy posing as a sex worker, it is possible that some had never before sought out a sex worker or had not successfully completed the transaction.

19 Rape myths are attitudes that have been shown to support sexual violence against women. Rape myths are 'prejudicial, stereotyped, or false beliefs about rape, rape victims, and rapists' (Burt, 1980: 217) that serve to justify or support sexual violence against women and diminish support for rape victims. They include the idea that women who are raped are in some way responsible for the violence against them, the idea that women often lie about being raped for selfish reasons, and the idea that only sexually promiscuous women are raped.

20 The choice of the number of factors is based on the number of eigenvalues of pattern/correlation matrix, which is the covariance matrix of the standardised variables, which are greater than 1. Eigenvalues for a certain factor measures the variance in all the variables, which are grouped into that factor. The ratio of eigenvalues is the ratio of explanatory importance of the factors with respect to the variables. A low eigenvalue poorly explains the variance of the variable. Thus, the correlation between indicators and factors is characterised by large loadings above 0.5, moderate loadings between 0.3 and 0.5 and small loadings below 0.3. In our case we have considered only loadings > 0.45.

21 'The desire to "have a variety of sexual partners" and "be in control during sex", and the need to "have sex immediately when I am aroused" all point to this kind of self-focused sexuality that Blanchard (1994) calls "McSex" in his popular expose on "young johns". According to one man he interviewed lt's like going to McDonalds; most people are looking for a good quick cheap meal. It's satisfying, it's greasy, and then you get the hell out of there'. Paying for sex because of the desire to have sex with women with particular physical attributes, a motivation described by McKeganey (1994), also reflects a conception of sex as a commodity' (Monto, 2000: 34).

22 Available from the authors on request.

23 We note that the distribution of the dependent variable is such that the percentage of 0, i.e. clients who use the condom never and seldom, is only 5.6%.

24 The IOM counter-trafficking activities are geared toward the prevention of trafficking in persons, particularly women and children, and the protection of migrant's rights. They include information campaigns, counselling, conducting research on migrant trafficking, ensuring safe and dignified return as well as reintegration assistance to the victims, helping governments to improve their legal systems and technical capacities in order to counter trafficking.

25 'Protocol to Prevent, Suppress and Punish Trafficking in Persons, Especially Women and Children' and 'Protocol Against the Smuggling of Migrants by Land, Sea and Air', supplementing the 'Convention Against Transnational Organized Crime'.

26 On the contrary, often, in the political discourse, the fight against trafficking is equated to a fight against sex work (Di Tommaso, 2007).

For instance, the United States Leadership Against HIV/AIDS, Tuberculosis and Malaria Act of 2003 sets aside US$15 billion in aid, but only to those organisations (for instance NGO's) that have an explicit policy opposing prostitution and sex trafficking (as if they were synonymous). No funds can be used to promote or advocate the legalisation or practice of prostitution or sex-trafficking. 'Included are organisation advocating prostitution as an employment choice or which advocate or support the legalisation of prostitution.' (Day and Ward, 2005: 157).

27 Once selected the variables for the estimates and deleted the cases where at least one variable was missing, our sample did not contain any men.

28 The transition matrix was constructed using the variable 'nationality' and the variable 'country agreed to work'. The total number of observations is 2499.

References

Akerlof, G. (1980). A theory of social custom, of which unemployment may be one consequence. *Quarterly Journal of Economics*, **94**(4): 749–775.

Aggleton, P. (Ed.) (1998). *Men Who Sell Sex*. London: UCL Press.

Arnott, R. and Stiglitz, J. E. (1991). *Equilibrium in Insurance Markets with Moral Hazard*. Working Paper No. 3588. Cambridge, MA: National Bureau of Economic Research,Inc.

Ben-Israel, H. and Levenkron, N. (2005). *The Missing Factor: Clients of Trafficked Women in Israel's Sex Industry*. unpublished manuscript, Hebrew University in Jerusalem.

Bindel, J. (2003). Tackling the traffickers. *Guardian*, 12 August.

Bordieu, P. (1986). *The Forms of Capital*. In Richardson J. G. (Ed.) *Handbook of Theory and Research for the Sociology of Education*, pp. 241–258. Greenwood.

Blanchard, K. (1995). Young Johns. *Mademoiselle*, **100**(5).

Burt, M. R. (1980). Cultural myths and supports for rape. *Journal of Personality and Social Psychology*, **38**: 1217–1230.

Cameron, S. (2002). *Economics of Sin: Rational Choice or No Choice at All?* Cheltenham: Edward Elgar Publishing Limited.

Cameron, S. and Collins, A. (2003). Estimates of a model of male participation in the market for female heterosexual prostitution services. *European Journal of Law and Economics*, **16**(3): 271–288.

Cameron, S., Collins, A. and Thew, N. (1999). Prostitution services: an exploratory empirical analysis. *Applied Economics*, **31**: 1523–1529.

Casson, M. (1991). *The Economics of Business Culture*. Oxford: Clarendon Press.

Coleman, J. S. (1988). Social capital in the creation of human capital. *American Journal of Sociology*, **94**: S95–S120.

Collins, A. (Ed.) (2004). Sex and the city. *Urban Studies,* **41**(9).

Corso, C. and Trifiro, A. (2003). *E Siamo Partite: Migrazione, tratta e prostituzione straniera in Italia*. Firenze; Giunti.

Day, S. and Ward (2004). *Sex, Work, Mobility, and Health in Europe*. USA: Kegal Paul Limited.

Di Tommaso, M. L., Shima, I., Strøm, S. and Bettio, F. (2007). *As Bad as it Gets: Well Being Deprivation of Sexually Exploited Trafficked Women Child* n. 10/2007. http://www.child-centre.it

Doezema, J. (1998). Forced to choose beyond the voluntary v. forced prostitution dichotomy. In Kempadoo, K. and Doezema, J. (Eds.), *Global Sex Workers: Rights, Resistance, and Redefinition*. New York and London: Routledge.

Edlund, L. and Korn E. (2002). An economic theory of prostitution. *Journal of Political Economy*, **110**(1).

Gallagher, A. (2001). Human rights and the new UN protocols on trafficking and migrant smuggling: a preliminary assessment. *Human Rights Quarterly*, **23**: 974–1004.

Garofalo, G. (2002). Towards an economic theory of prostitution, *mimeo*, University of Siena.

Gertler *et al.* (2003). Risky Business: the market for unprotected prostitution. *mimeo*, Cornell University.

Goleman, D. (1996). *Emotional Intelligence*. London: Bloomsbury Publishing.

Granovetter, M. (1985). Economic action and social structure: the problem of embeddedness. *American Journal of Sociology*, **91**: 481–510.

Harding, S. (1986). *The Science Question in Feminism*. Ithaca and London: Cornell University Press Scott.

Hirsch, F. (1977). *Social Limits to Growth*. London: Routledge & Kegan Paul.

Kempadoo, K. and Doezema, J. (Eds.) (1998). *Global Sex Workers: Rights, Resistance, and Redefinition*. London: Routledge.

Kern, R. M. (2000). Prostitute client profiles: indicators of motivations for prostitution use, *mimeo*, Eastern Michigan University.

Kuo, L. (2002). *Prostitution Policy: Revolutionizing Practice through a Gendered Perspective*. New York and London: New York University Press.

Lim, L. L. (Ed.) (1998). *The Sex Sector: The Economic and Social Bases of Prostitution in Southeast Asia*. Geneva: International Labour Office.

Mansky, C. (2000). Economic analysis of social interactions. *Journal of Economic Perspectives*, **14**: 114–136.

Marttila, A. M. (2003). Consuming sex: Finnish male clients and Russian and Baltic prostitution. Presented at *Gender and Power in the New Europe, the 5th European Feminist Research Conference August 20–24, 2003*. Lund University, Sweden.

McKeganey, N. and Barnard, M. (1996). *Sex Work on the Streets: Sex Workers and their Clients*. Buckingham: Open University Press.

Moffat, P. G. and Peters, S. A. (2001). The pricing of personal services, *mimeo*, Royal Economic Society in Durham.

Monto, M. A. (2000a). *Clients of Street Sex Workers in Portland, Oregon, San Francisco and Santa Clara, California, and Las Vegas, Nevada, 1996–1999*, University of Portland. Ann Arbor, MI: Inter-University Consortium for Political and Social Research.

Monto, M. (2000b). Why men seek out sex workers. In R. Weitzer (Ed.), *Sex for Sale: Prostitution, Pornography, and the Sex Industry*. New York: Routledge.

Munro, V. and Della Giusta, M. (Eds.) (2008). *Interrogating Supply/Demand Dynamics in Prostitution*. London: Ashgate.

Nussbaum, M. (1999). *Sex and Social Justice*. New York: Oxford University Press.

O'Connell Davidson, J. (1998). *Prostitution Power and Freedom*. Cambridge: Polity Press.

O'Connell Davidson, J. (2001). *The Rights and Wrongs of Prostitution*. **17**(2): 84–96.

O'Connell Davidson, J. (2002). *Trafficking — A Demand-Led Problem?* Stockholm: Save the Children Sweden.

O'Connell Davidson, J. and Anderson, B. (2006). The trouble with "trafficking". In Van der Anker, C. L. and Doomernick, J. (Eds.), *Trafficking and Women's Rights*. UK: Polgrave (Macmillan).

O'Kane, M. (2002). *Prostitution: The Laws Don't Work*. Channel 4 Documentary, UK.

Outshoorn, J. (Ed.) (2004). *The Politics of Prostitution: Women's Movements, Democratic States, and the Globalization of Sex Commerce*. Cambridge University Press.

Pagano, U. (1989). *The Politics and the Economics of Power*. London: Routledge.

Pateman, C. (1988). *The Sexual Contract*. Polity Press, Cambridge and Stanford University Press.

Pitts, M. K., Smith, A. M. A., O'Brien, M. and Misson, S. (2004). Who pays for sex and why? An analysis of social and motivational factors associated with male clients of sex workers. *Archives of Sexual Behaviour*, **33**(4): 353–358.

Putnam, R. (1993). *Making Democracy Work: Civic Traditions in Modern Italy*. Princeton University Press.

Radin, M. J. (1996). *Contested Commodities*. Cambridge, MA: Harvard University Press.

Rao, V., Gupta, I., Lokshin, M. and Jana, S. (2003). Sex workers and the cost of safe sex: the compensating differential for condom use among Calcutta sex workers. *Journal of Development Economics*, **71**: 585–603.

Reynolds, H. (1986). *The Economics of Prostitution*. Illinois, IL: Thomas.

Rubin, G. (1975). The traffic in women: notes on the "Political Economy" of Sex. In Reiter, R. (Ed.), *Towards an Anthropology of Women*, pp. 157–210, New York: Monthly Review Press.

Ryley Scott, G. (1976). *A History of Prostitution form Antiquity to Present Day*. New York: AMS Press.

Sanchez Taylor, J. (2001). Dollars are a girls' best friend? female tourists' sexual behaviour in the Caribbean. *Sociology*, **35**(3): 749–764. Cambridge: Cambridge University Press.

Sullivan, E. and Simon, W. (1998). The client: a social, psychological, and behavioural look at the unseen patron of prostitution. In Elias, J. E. and Brewer, G. (Eds.), *Prostitution*. New York: Prometheus Books.

Thorbek, S. and Pattanaik, B. (Eds.) (2002). *Transnational Prostitution: Changing Global Patterns*. London: Zed Books.

Tiggey, M., Harocopos, A. and Hough, M. (2000). *For Love or Money: Pimps and the Management of Sex Work*. London: Home Office, Policing and Reducing Crime Unit.

UNDP (2006). *Human Development Report*. United Nations Development Program.

United Nations (2000). *Protocol to Prevent, Supress, and Punish Trafficking in Persons, Especially in Women and Children.*

UNODC (2006). *Trafficking in Persons: Global Patterns*. UNODC, Vienna.

Ward, H. (2008). Abolitionism in the UK. In Munro, V. and Della Giusta, M. (Eds.), *The Supply/Demand Dynamic in Prostitution*. Aldershot: Ashgate.

Index

Printed in the United States
by Baker & Taylor Publisher Services